ISSUES THAT CONCERN YOU

Exercise and Fitness

Laurie Willis, *Book Editor*

GREENHAVEN PRESS
A part of Gale, Cengage Learning

GALE
CENGAGE Learning·

Detroit • New York • San Francisco • New Haven, Conn • Waterville, Maine • London

Elizabeth Des Chenes, *Director, Publishing Solutions*

© 2013 Greenhaven Press, a part of Gale, Cengage Learning

Gale and Greenhaven Press are registered trademarks used herein under license.

For more information, contact:
Greenhaven Press
27500 Drake Rd.
Farmington Hills, MI 48331-3535
Or you can visit our Internet site at gale.cengage.com

For product information and technology assistance, contact us at

Gale Customer Support, 1-800-877-4253
For permission to use material from this text or product, submit all requests online at www.cengage.com/permissions

Further permissions questions can be e-mailed to permissionrequest@cengage.com

Articles in Greenhaven Press anthologies are often edited for length to meet page requirements. In addition, original titles of these works are changed to clearly present the main thesis and to explicitly indicate the author's opinion. Every effort is made to ensure that Greenhaven Press accurately reflects the original intent of the authors. Every effort has been made to trace the owners of copyrighted material.

Cover image © Andresr/Shutterstock.com.

LIBRARY OF CONGRESS CATALOGING-IN-PUBLICATION DATA

Exercise and fitness / Laurie Willis, book editor.
    p. cm. -- (Issues that concern you)
Includes bibliographical references and index.
ISBN 978-0-7377-6293-8 (hardcover)
1. Physical fitness for children. 2. Exercise for children--Physiological aspects.
3. Obesity in children. I. Willis, Laurie, editor of compilation.
RJ133.E935 2013
613.7042--dc23
                                            2012034553

Printed in the United States of America
1 2 3 4 5 6 7 16 15 14 13 12

CONTENTS

Television "screen time" has long been pointed to as one of the causes of childhood obesity. As computers and video games entered the market, they too started to be blamed for a decline in physical activity. However, not everyone believes screen time is the main cause of lack of physical fitness in children. In the February 2004 issue of the *Journal of Adolescence*, the authors of a University of Texas study on the relationships between childhood obesity and use of television and video games state,

> It would be wonderful if there were a quick and easy solution to the problem of obesity in American youth. Unfortunately, the data available to date do not support the notion that turning off the television or unplugging the video game console amounts to a "magic bullet" which will reduce the prevalence of childhood obesity. As with most other phenomena, the data point to a complex and interrelated pattern of factors contributing to obesity in children and adolescents.

With the rise of game systems like Nintendo's Wii and Microsoft's Xbox Kinect and of active games such as *Dance Dance Revolution* (sometimes known as "exergames"), some have started to point to video games as part of the solution to childhood obesity, rather than part of the problem. In the results of a 2011 University of Utah study, Bruce Bailey and Kyle McInnis write, "Exergaming has the potential to increase physical activity and have a favorable influence on energy balance, and may be a viable alternative to traditional fitness activities." Bonnie Mohnsen, who operates an online business that provides schools with technological tools to improve physical education programs, agrees. "Exercise can be boring and routine," she says. "Why not motivate [students] to move the body by playing a game?"

However, a 2011 study by Tom Baranowski and others, reported in the journal *Pediatrics*, suggests that the solution is not so simple. This study attempted to determine whether having access

Exercise video games like Your Shape *have been touted as part of the solution to childhood obesity.*

to active video games would encourage children to be more physically active. The authors indicate "that simply acquiring a new active video game does not automatically lead to increased PA [physical activity], thereby minimizing the public health value of simply having active video games available for children to play." Also, a new repetitive strain injury caused by repeated motions while playing an active video game has been dubbed "Nintendinitis," according to the *Medical Journal of Australia.*

The relationship between video games and fitness has inspired much debate, as have numerous other topics related to exercise and fitness. Some of the viewpoints in *Issues That Concern You: Exercise and Fitness* discuss general attitudes about the causes of obesity. Others consider how nutrition and eating behaviors affect fitness. Several of the viewpoints focus on exercise, including

Michelle Obama's Let's Move! program, and physical education classes in schools. The final selections consider the impact of sports injuries on young people. In addition, the volume contains several appendixes to help the reader understand and explore the topic, including a thorough bibliography and a list of organizations to contact for further information. The appendix titled "What You Should Know About Exercise and Fitness" offers facts about obesity, eating habits, exercise, and the link between physical education and academic performance. The appendix "What You Should Do About Exercise and Fitness" offers tips for young people on conducting research on the issue, evaluating sources, and taking action to improve personal fitness or establish programs at school or in the community. With all these features, *Issues That Concern You: Exercise and Fitness* provides a thorough resource for those interested in this issue.

ONE

Teenagers Are Too Sedentary

Josephine Marcotty

A 2008 study of adolescents in cities across the United States showed that there is a dramatic drop in the level of physical activity around age thirteen for girls and fourteen and a half for boys. In this viewpoint Josephine Marcotty, a reporter for the *Minneapolis Star Tribune*, discusses this study. She notes that most of the teens who remain active are members of competitive sports teams. Experts recommend that a larger variety of athletic opportunities should be offered for teens who are not involved with team sports.

New research is charting the roots of the nation's obesity epidemic: Between the ages of 9 and 15, kids' daily physical activity drops from an average of three hours to less than one.

On weekends it's worse. Fifteen-year-olds, on average, move around only 35 minutes a day on Saturdays and Sundays, according to a study of 1,000 kids across the country. The results, published today [July 16, 2008] in the *Journal of the American Medical Association (JAMA)*, put physicians on notice that they need to pay more attention to whether their young patients are spending too much time online and on their cell phones, and not enough at the pool or park.

"There is a lot of pressure on physicians to start addressing this," said Dan Halvorsen, an expert in pediatric exercise physiology at the University of Minnesota.

It is the latest in a year of alarming news about childhood obesity and the diseases that come with it. Nearly a third of the nation's kids are too heavy and increasingly sedentary. Just last week [July

Children's activity levels drop off from three to just one hour a day between the ages of nine and fifteen, according to a study cited by the author.

2008] the American Academy of Pediatrics caused consternation among doctors and parents when it issued guidelines for more aggressive use of cholesterol drugs in at-risk children to protect them from the heart disease they may have later in life.

National health guidelines recommend that both teenagers and adults get at least an hour of moderate physical activity every day. As the study published this week shows, most teenagers have a long way to go.

Activity Drops Rapidly as Teens Grow Older

The study also reveals at what ages doctors have to start paying attention to the drop in activity—around age 13 for girls and 14½ for boys. That's when the amount of time spent being physically active drops precipitously.

"What shocked me was the dramatic decline. It drops off really fast," said Dr. Philip Nader, a pediatric cardiology researcher at the University of California, San Diego, who conducted the study.

Most research studies that track kids' physical activity rely on surveys and reports by the kids themselves, which, as any parent knows, can be rather inaccurate. Nader did it differently.

He and his fellow researchers put an accelerometer—a device that measures physical movement—on a total of about 1,000 kids in 10 different cities. . . . The kids wore it on their waist for seven days while it logged how much they biked, walked, jumped or sat around.

The younger they were, the more active they were. Nine-year-olds logged an average of three hours a day of moderate to vigorous activity. By age 12 that had dropped to about an hour and a half on weekdays and 83 minutes on weekends. By age 15 it was down to 49 minutes during the week and 35 minutes on the weekends. At every age, boys were somewhat more active than girls.

At age 15 only 28 percent of kids were physically active for an hour or more each weekday. On weekends the rate dropped to 14 percent.

Dr. Angela Fitch, a pediatrician with the Fairview Eagan Clinic, sees ways kids are socializing and using technology that explain the study's findings.

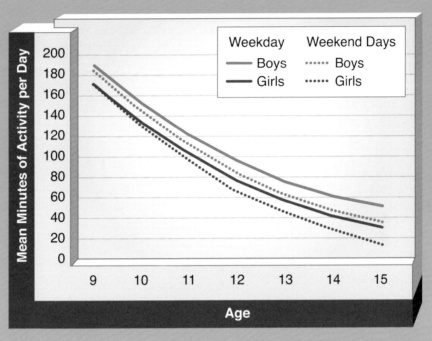

Average Minutes of Physical Activity for Boys and Girls

	Weekday	Weekend Days
Boys	——	······
Girls	——	······

Mean Minutes of Activity per Day
(200, 180, 160, 140, 120, 100, 80, 60, 40, 20, 0)

Age (9, 10, 11, 12, 13, 14, 15)

Taken from: P.R. Nader, et al. "Moderate-to-Vigorous Physical Activity from Ages 9 to 15 Years." *JAMA*, July 16, 2008.

She said a co-worker recently recounted a moment that would be familiar to many parents in the age of texting, e-mail and instant messaging. The co-worker's 12-year-old daughter came home early from a school dance and went straight to the computer to message her friends. When her parents asked why she didn't go over to someone's house or have a sleepover, she replied: "'We don't have to. We can talk like this,'" Fitch said. "Instead of pillow fighting they are sitting in front of a computer messaging each other."

Kids Not on Sports Teams Stop Being Active

Halvorsen said that the kids who keep moving are often the ones who make it to increasingly elite sports teams. Officials from the

Minnesota State High School League estimate that about 38 percent of the state's 253,000 10th- through 12th-graders participate in at least one sport at school—one of the highest participation rates in the country. But that still leaves 62 percent of high school students needing other ways to be active.

"Right around the ages of 12, 13 or 14, the fun sports are becoming competitive sports," Halvorsen said. The kids who make it onto the athletic sports teams tend to stay active, he said. "Sadly, the rest of them don't have many options."

Kids would benefit if schools and community organizations started offering more varieties of organized sports—everything from table tennis to ultimate frisbee—for the kids who don't choose traditional sports such as hockey or basketball, Halvorsen said.

Ultimately, exercise has to be a family affair, and in order for it to become a lifelong habit it has to start before adolescence, said Dr. Gigi Chawla, a pediatrician at Children's Hospital in St. Paul.

"You can't just expect your child to go out to the park and run around while you watch," she said. "You need to bike to the park together."

TWO

Schools Should Take Charge of Student Fitness

David Satcher

David Satcher served as surgeon general of the United States from 1998 to 2001. In this viewpoint he discusses the current levels of obesity and other health issues among students and calls upon schools to take a leadership role in helping students become healthier. He describes several innovative programs conducted by schools that are proving to be successful, and he recommends that schools partner with parents and communities to help improve student health.

While serving as U.S. surgeon general in 2001, I released *The Surgeon General's Call to Action to Prevent and Decrease Overweight and Obesity*. This report concluded that the sharp increase in the rate of overweight and obesity between 1980 and 2000 had touched all ethnic groups and threatened to become the leading cause of preventable death in the United States.

Because of schools' unique ability to open doors of opportunity for all youngsters, regardless of their socioeconomic backgrounds or ethnicity, educators have an essential role to play in advancing student health and preventing childhood obesity. If we want all our children to have an equal chance to succeed in school and in life, our schools must not only promote academic achievement but also help students develop habits of healthy eating and physical activity.

An Unhealthy Start to the Twenty-First Century

More than 30 percent of children ages 2–19 in the United States are overweight or obese. In the past three decades, this rate has doubled among U.S. preschool and adolescent children and tripled among 6- to 11-year-olds.

Regardless of race and socioeconomic status, overweight children are more likely to become overweight adults. This is not a cosmetic issue, but a serious health threat. Overweight individuals are at increased risk of developing cardiovascular disease, diabetes, and certain cancers.

Unfortunately, both adults and children increasingly overeat and eat the wrong foods. Trends contributing to obesity include more restaurant dining and the proliferation of microwaves and processed foods. According to the U.S. Department of Agriculture, few school-age children eat well, consuming the recommended daily amounts of fruits, vegetables, and whole grains as well as low-fat and nonfat dairy products to strengthen bones and build healthy bodies. Children and youth in poor communities—which often have limited or no access to fresh fruits and vegetables, along with other disparities—are especially vulnerable.

Equally disturbing is the fact that young people are not moving enough, at home or at school. The Centers for Disease Control and Prevention found that about 62 percent of children ages 9–13 did not participate in any organized physical activity during their nonschool hours, and 23 percent did not engage in any free-time physical activity. Black and Hispanic children were significantly less likely than non-Hispanic white children to report involvement in organized activities, as were children with parents who had lower incomes and education levels. And few schools offer daily physical education throughout the academic year—only 4 percent of elementary schools, 8 percent of middle schools, and 2 percent of high schools.

Poor Health Affects Learning

A growing body of evidence shows that children who eat poorly or who engage in too little physical activity do not perform as well as they could academically. Poor nutrition affects students' learning in a number of ways, depriving them of essential vitamins, minerals, fats, and proteins that are necessary for optimal cognitive function.

Research also suggests the benefits of improving students' nutrition and physical activity. One body of research has examined the effects of giving students a healthy nutritional start to the day through school breakfast programs. Numerous studies have

Percentage of Schools Nationwide That Require Physical Education in Each Grade

Grade	% of All Schools
Kindergarten	49.7
1st	57.2
2nd	57.7
3rd	58.0
4th	58.2
5th	61.1
6th	68.1
7th	67.1
8th	65.5
9th	55.3
10th	33.2
11th	20.2
12th	20.4

Taken from: Sarah M. Lee et al. "Physical Education and Physical Activity: Results from the School Health Policies and Programs Study 2006." *Journal of School Health*, October 2007.

found that increased participation in school breakfast programs is associated with increases in test scores, daily attendance, and class participation, as well as reduced absenteeism and tardiness.

A meta-analysis of about 200 studies found that regular physical activity can promote learning. Data from one study showed that participation in a two-year, health-related physical education program significantly improved academic achievement.

Only a handful of studies have examined the relationship between being overweight and learning. However, common sense tells us that overweight students face a number of barriers to school success. Being overweight can trigger or exacerbate a variety of chronic medical conditions—including asthma, type 2 diabetes, high blood pressure, depression and anxiety, and sleep apnea—that increase school absentee rates.

In addition to missing school, children who are overweight often face psychological and social problems that inhibit their academic performance. For example, one study found a strong association between being overweight in kindergarten and behavior problems such as anxiety, loneliness, low self-esteem, sadness, anger, excessive arguing, and fighting.

New Policies Achieve Limited Success

A promising first step toward improving student health in the United States occurred in 2004, when Congress passed the Child Nutrition and WIC Reauthorization Act. This act required all schools with federally funded school meal programs to develop local wellness policies by the 2006 academic year.

Unfortunately, policies on the books do not necessarily translate into effective practices. Although the majority of U.S. schools have adopted policies to address poor nutrition and physical inactivity, many significant and serious gaps remain in local school wellness efforts. According to Action for Healthy Kids' 2008 report, *Progress or Promises? What's Working For and Against Healthy Schools*, many of these policies are weakly written and implemented. Most students still lack access to healthy, kid-appealing food choices.

Although schools have made progress in removing junk foods from the campus, they have been less successful in providing nutritious options that students will actually choose to eat, especially whole grains, low-fat and nonfat dairy, fruits, and vegetables. The report also found a lack of engagement with school wellness among school leaders, teachers, students, and parents.

Innovative Programs Are Making a Difference

Although daunting hurdles and gaps persist, the good news is that many exciting and encouraging interventions are making a positive difference in schools across the United States. Here are just a few examples.

In Michigan, health and education leaders collaborated on a Web site (http://mihealthtools.org/schoolsuccess) featuring real-world stories of local schools successfully building healthier environments. One of the more than 300 examples is the Walking and Pedometer Club at Burton Elementary and Middle School in Grand Rapids. Three days a week, approximately 150 students walk or run about a mile a day; students who log 15 miles or more receive a reward. Teachers and other staff members volunteer to monitor the program and record student progress. The school reports that since it has implemented the club, students are calmer in class and fewer students visit the health office.

The Web site contains many more examples of practical ways to advance school wellness, such as incorporating exercise breaks into classroom time, holding school-wide physical activity events, implementing Farm-to-School programs to use local produce in school lunches, and involving families in healthy eating.

Action for Healthy Kids has developed a program called Students Taking Charge, which motivates, educates, and empowers high school students to improve their personal health and to instigate wellness improvements in their school. Supported by a Web site (www.studentstakingcharge.org) and program volunteers, students develop and lead youth summits and peer-mentor training opportunities. As part of the Students Taking Charge video contest, students in 12 states created videos that

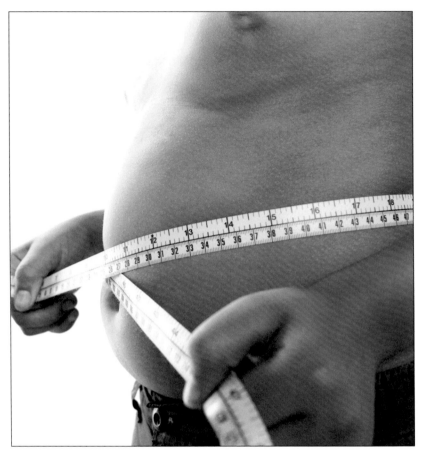

In the United States more than 30 percent of children aged two to nineteen are overweight or obese.

were posted on YouTube showing why their schools are healthy places to learn.

In February 2009, Houston Independent School District in Texas held the Healthy Kids, Healthy Schools summit, launching a collaborative, whole-system change initiative with leadership support from more than 80 local, state, and national organizations (www.healthykidshealthyschools.org). The full community of stakeholders—business leaders, government officials, parents, health professionals, students, community leaders, school administrators and educators—have come together to create healthier schools in Houston.

Beginning in the 2009–10 school year, these volunteers are implementing a range of projects focused on improving nutrition and opportunities for physical activity. For example, one project team is working on increasing students' access to healthy, appealing foods. The plan includes introducing a new, healthy pizza product in school lunches, accompanied by promotions and nutrition education tie-ins, as well as expanding the district's Grab-n-Go Carts program to increase access to and consumption of kid-appealing fruits, vegetables, low-fat milk, and whole grain products. The carts project will be piloted in four school cafeterias with items attractively priced to encourage students to try healthier foods.

Another team is working on increasing community support and resources. Its plan includes a Healthy Food Zones initiative that encourages local businesses and stores around schools to offer healthy food options to students.

Everyone Should Work Together to Promote Health

Poor nutrition and physical inactivity harm the well-being and academic performance of students. To ensure the brightest future possible for our children, more educators, policymakers, community leaders, businesses, and parents need to embrace and advocate for proactive school health programs. By working together, we can ensure that every student enjoys a learning environment that not only supports academic achievement but also promotes lifelong habits of physical activity and proper nutrition.

THREE

Families Should Take Charge of Kids' Fitness

Susan J. Grosse

> Susan J. Grosse is past president of the American Association for Active Lifestyles and Fitness. In this viewpoint she recommends that families make fitness a priority. She suggests a number of ideas for family fitness, including taking walks together, backyard play, and keeping fitness activities interesting by turning them into challenges.

Daily lives are busy times. Work and school take up a big chunk. Daily care of a child with a disability can be time consuming. Television and computer use increasingly dominate leisure. Meals are often on the run. Family members pass each other, as each strives to keep up the pace. Given magical wishes, most individuals would wish for increased family togetherness time.

Living at a fast pace can also mean some aspects of a healthy lifestyle can be overlooked. Obesity, heart disease, diabetes, and a host of other health impairments are on the rise. Many can be attributed to lack of exercise. A second magical wish of families is improved opportunities for development and maintenance of physical fitness. Here's how your family can have both—togetherness AND fitness.

First, make family fitness a priority. Yes, schedules are packed full. You cannot do everything. However, the values and priorities you set for your family now will be the foundation supporting your children for the rest of their lives. Health depends, in large part, on fitness. Life-guiding values are imparted through family interaction. Blend the two to give your child the very best start while at the same time contributing to your own wellness.

Walking, backyard games, and fitness challenges are three easy ways to implement family friendly activities for improving and maintaining physical health.

Biking, walking, having fitness challenges, and playing family backyard games are four easy ways to implement family-friendly activities for improving and maintaining physical fitness, says the author.

Family Walks Can Be Fun

A family walk is a great time to bond with your child, as well as integrate fitness. Don't just stroll. Set a brisk pace. Let the arms swing. It's fine to get a bit out of breath. Don't slow down for hills or stairs. Walk around the block, through the mall, from the farthest parking space (rather than closest), or through the woods. Walk in the museum, at the zoo, to the store, and to the post office. One thousand steps per day are recognized as a good fitness goal.

Remember, the walk is family time. Everyone should have a say in destination. Everyone should have a chance to interact with other family members while walking. This means leave the iPod at home and carry on [a] conversation. Ask your child questions about his or her day, what you are seeing along the walk, or about current events. As long as everyone can talk while they walk, the exertion level is appropriate. Ask riddles, sing songs, and chant rhymes. Kick objects along the way or take along a tennis ball to bounce or toss back and forth. Become collectors. Watch for pretty leaves or unusual stones. Pick up litter.

Stretch your mind while you walk. Do the math by counting steps, estimating how many steps to a specific destination, or comparing strides of different family members. Read street names and call [out] words that rhyme with them. Take along a compass or make a map as you go.

Does this mean a walk should be planned? Yes, to some extent. Just walking is not family bonding (and sitting at home talking is not a fitness activity). Walk with a purpose: fitness for the whole family.

Backyards Provide a Place for Family Games

That patch of grass, sidewalk, or driveway next to your house or apartment building can be a great place for family fitness. Fitness means developing flexibility from moving in many different directions, increasing endurance from continuing an activity even when tired, building strength from moving increasingly heavier objects, and fostering cardiorespiratory function by raising the heart rate and maintaining that increased rate for at least 10 min-

"But it's a beautiful day and all of the other Moms are outside and..."

utes at a time. If you don't have anything useful as a backyard, head for a neighborhood park.

Chalk can be used to mark the cement or blacktop for hopscotch or four-square. A rope strung between two trees, poles, or hooks on buildings can substitute for a net. Over that net you can toss and catch a ball or pillow; play badminton; volley a beach ball, balloon, or volleyball; or throw and catch a Frisbee. Save milk cartons. Fill them with water. Now you have obstacles you can place on the ground for running zig-zag patterns, dribbling a soccer ball, or suspending low level rope hurdles.

You don't need expensive sports equipment for backyard family fitness. Making or improvising equipment can be part of this family friendly activity, thus fostering problem solving and creativity in your child, as well as that sense of accomplishment everyone will have upon completion of a fun activity.

Take a look in your garage. What can you use to make an obstacle course? Crawling under lawn chairs, running around a hose rack, and climbing over a pile of newspapers tied up for trash collection can provide challenges for everyone when performance is timed and family members race. Make sure all equipment is activity friendly, with no sharp edges or dangerous protrusions. Have everyone wear old clothes and spend family fitness time out in your own backyard.

Challenges Can Make Fitness Interesting

A challenge is measured performance. A challenge answers the questions "How many?" or "How fast?" or "How far?" Make a chart, explain the challenge, select a time to perform the challenge of the day, and see who can be the challenge champ during any given week. Here are examples of fitness challenges for the whole family, including some for those who use a wheelchair.

- How many can-ups can you do in a minute? (Take two identical cans of food, place one can in each hand and then lift both cans overhead till elbows are straight and then back to shoulders for one "can-up".)
- How close to touching your toes can you get when sitting on the floor with legs straight out in front of you with knees straight or when sitting in a wheelchair and bending at the waist?
- How far can you underhand toss a beanbag?
- How many push-ups can you do in 30 seconds?
- How many times can you go up and down the stairs in two minutes?

- How fast can you get from the basement to the top floor and back down again?
- How high can you jump and reach against a wall? (From a standing position with your side next to the wall and near arm extended overhead, jump and reach as high as you can.)
- How far can you seal walk? (Lying on your stomach, push up on your arms until your arms are straight and then walk on your hands, dragging the rest of your body.)

Fitness doesn't just happen. Even individuals with very active lives may not be getting activities appropriate for developing each of the major fitness components of flexibility, strength, endurance, and cardiorespiratory function. Planning family fitness activities means being sure all areas of fitness are included.

By the same token, family bonding also doesn't just happen. Passing family members as each goes in and out of the house or stops in the kitchen for a snack isn't bonding. Fitness development and family bonding require interaction and communication. Structure fitness activities so all family members can participate and gain the best of both—a physically fit family that not only works, but also plays as a family. That's a family putting down a great foundation for every family member's future.

FOUR

Communities and Families Should Take Responsibility for Healthy Diets

Deborah Douglas

> In some neighborhoods, known as "food deserts," grocery stores do not offer many healthy options, because these do not sell as well as snacks and sodas. In this viewpoint from the National Association for the Advancement of Colored People's the *Crisis*, a journal focusing on issues facing African American and other people of color, journalist Deborah Douglas discusses the makeup of these neighborhoods—usually African American and Latino—and notes that these populations also suffer from many of the health risks that are made worse by poor diets. She applauds First Lady Michelle Obama's Let's Move! fitness campaign and urges communities and families to take more responsibility for the foods consumed by their children.

Handing out literature recently at a Sam's Club [warehouse store] in suburban Chicago, Curves fitness franchisee Kimberley Rudd had an eye-opening conversation with the store's White manager:

Deborah Douglas, "The War Against Obesity," *The Crisis*, Spring 2010, pp. 26–30. Copyright © 2010 by Crisis Publishing Co., Inc. All rights reserved. Reproduced by permission. Gale/Cengage Learning wishes to thank the Crisis Publishing Co., Inc., the publisher of the magazine of the National Association for the Advancement of Colored People, for the use of the material first published in the Spring 2010 issue of *The Crisis*.

He told me, "We don't carry a lot of healthy food in here. We have fresh produce, but it's not a big section. I'll be honest with you: Most of my customers are African American. When I put Diet Pepsi at the front of the store, it just stays there. But when I put Little Hugs up front," which is basically sugar-water wrapped in plastic, "they're blowing right through them. Diet cookies, granola bars? They don't sell here. My customers like sugar. This is interesting to me because a lot of my customers also buy a lot of diabetic supplies. They're diabetics who love sugar."

In many corners of Black America, life is about subsisting on artificially flavored fruit drinks, anything topped with melted cheese and astronomical portions. Squeeze into a seat on a crowded city bus or train during rush-hour traffic lately? Stood in line at the neighborhood chicken shack on payday? Attended a Black church? Anyone making the rounds of Black life in America with their eyes wide open can see the obvious:

Black folks are among the fattest people in America.

Of course, overweight and obese adults who reject the lifestyle changes necessary to fight the fat can do whatever they please. If [comedienne and actress] Mo'Nique's man likes her big 'n' curvy, who are we to criticize? But overweight kids who can't or won't move and increasingly show signs of adult diseases such as clogged arteries and stroke—now that's a problem.

Here are the facts: Just as African Americans are disproportionately affected by job loss, home foreclosures, sub-prime loans and food stamp use, they are No. 1 in f-a-t. Latinos aren't much better off. American obesity rates have tripled, and at any given moment, nearly 36 percent of African Americans are considered obese. Almost 29 percent of Latinos' body mass index scores qualify them as obese. White Americans are tipping the scales too: 23.7 percent of them are obese. Experts predict nearly 75 percent of Americans will be overweight and 41 percent of them will be obese by 2015.

The stats on our children aren't easy on the eye, either: The prevalence of excess weight jumped more than 120 percent among Black and Latino children between 1986 and 1998, according to a national study; and more than 50 percent among White children. The numbers on the Centers for Disease Control [and Prevention, CDC,] website show that from 1976–1980 to 2007–2008, the prevalence of obesity among children ages 6 to 11 tripled; for children ages 12 to 19, it more than tripled.

"Issues of racism and classism are associated with health diseases," says Shavon L. Arline, NAACP [National Association for the Advancement of Colored People] health programs director. "Depending on where you live, skin color can affect whether you have access to fruits and vegetables, whether you have access to physical education, not to mention having a safe and built environment so you can really enjoy pure play," says Arline, who holds a master of public health degree. Getting the nation's children to trim down will require a profound cultural shift, one in which Arline says the NAACP is engaged at the federal, state and local levels.

Tackling the country's obesity problem and the diseases that grow out of it (such as diabetes, heart disease, arthritis and cancer) demands an approach that will save all by ministering to the needs of those suffering most. And anyone who believes this oversize problem is too big to tackle should instead view it as one that's too big to fail. Besides, public health campaigns can be successful. Think: seatbelts.

"I was so thrilled when the first lady and the president [Michelle and Barack Obama] stood up to say, 'We're going to focus on this problem,'" says Jim Sallis, a San Diego State University psychology professor whose primary research interests include nutrition and obesity. "There had never been any strong leadership. There was never a nationally focused effort to do what needs to be done."

Although Michelle Obama is now the face of America's battle against childhood obesity, Sallis notes that the president has skin in the game, too. The same day that Mrs. Obama announced her Let's Move campaign, the president asked multiple government agencies, such as the Departments of Agriculture [USDA], Education and the Interior, to join a task force to develop anti-obesity policies and initiatives within their respective areas.

"These are government departments that had not been very involved in obesity prevention," Sallis says. "I am 100 percent supportive. All of us in the field appreciate her leadership."

Children Today Are Less Active than in the Past

This is an auspicious time for Mrs. Obama to launch her Let's Move campaign, designed to dial back childhood obesity by promoting healthy food choices, raising school food standards, and challenging and rewarding kids to lead more active lives. Despite all the aforementioned bad news, American obesity rates for children and adults are stabilizing, according to the Centers for Disease Control and Prevention. Obesity rates for most low-income, preschool-aged children, for example, leveled off, according to a 2009 CDC report.

Given the time constraints of working families, parents might believe they're already doing all they can to expose their children to healthy food and safe activity. But forces bigger than Mom and Dad contribute to children's expanded waistlines. Children are not nearly as active as their parents were when they were in school. While the presence of physical education classes hasn't proved to have a significant impact on trimming the fat, there is a quality issue afflicting America's gym classes. Moreover, while "food deserts," characterized by a fruitless search for healthful foods in nonexistent neighborhood grocery stores, affect Americans of all stripes, African Americans—the fattest Americans—are affected most.

As more schools teach to the test to boost scores and meet program standards, physical education often has been deemed irrelevant. The lack of physical education classes can be blamed directly for contributing to the childhood weight problem.

"When you talk to school administrators, the No Child Left Behind law requires a certain amount of time be spent on reading, math and that sort of thing," Sallis says. "The funding of their school is dependent on academic achievement, so everything else becomes secondary. We're pushing out physical education, cutting down on recess and spending as much time as possible on the topics that are covered on the test."

Frank Chaloupka, an economist at the University of Illinois at Chicago, agrees. "The bottom line is kids don't have the same access they had years ago," he says. "Physical activity has been crowded out by other competing demands. If you go back

Thirty-six percent of African Americans are considered obese, with diet directly linked to this obesity.

a few decades, kids had a regular recess and physical education classes. We're not seeing that today; a lot of kids have P.E. classes infrequently. Not everybody is required to take it in primary schools."

The duration of gym classes tends to decline over time, according to "Bridging the Gap," a series of studies by

Chaloupka and other researchers published in the *American Journal of Preventive Medicine*. In eighth grade, students spend an average of 172 minutes in gym class per week compared with 89 minutes by 12th grade. By then, only a third of students take a gym class during the school year, the study says. Likely because of fewer resources, minority students from lower socio-economic classes are also less involved in varsity sports by high school.

Gym teachers routinely complain about being sidelined, marginalized and the first to be laid off in a budget crunch. The students suffer just as much from their removal, Sallis says, because physical activity helps kids focus better on academics.

"Immediately after an activity break, kids are paying attention more," Sallis says. "They're concentrating more. This is why we're trying to get the word out about these kinds of studies. This is the kind of mechanism by which physical activity can have an immediate effect."

Healthy Foods Are Scarce in Food Deserts

Students who live in food deserts frequently encounter empty calories before they hit the schoolhouse doors. The lure of Flamin' Hots, soda and other salt- and sugar-laden food is irresistible, especially when few healthy alternatives are available.

"In Chicago, the vast majority of food desert residents are African American," says Mari Gallagher, whose Chicago-based firm has done groundbreaking work on which neighborhoods across the country have access to healthy food and why. "For both African Americans and Whites, if you live in one of these food deserts, there's a significant relationship between death and diabetes. There's many, many more African Americans who face that risk. And not everybody in a food desert is poor."

Gallagher was working in community development when she realized the connection between poor health and lack of mainstream food options. Even when residents prefer healthy foods, those who live in food deserts often find themselves compromising for themselves and their children by resorting to liquor or corner stores for quick-fix meals. Food deserts have been identified by the U.S. Economic Research Services in cities such as Detroit, Chicago, Los Angeles, Riverside, Calif., St. Louis, Denver and Atlanta.

Rudd, the Curves franchisee, wonders, however, if the food desert/health connection is a cop-out: "I run into plenty of people who go out to the mall, movies and family members' houses, but they can't get to a grocery store to buy fresh fruits and vegetables?"

She recalls a 13-year-old girl who came to work out over Christmas break. The girl weighed more than 200 pounds. When asked who does the cooking and shopping in her household, she said her mother does it all. When asked if she insists on putting cookies in the grocery basket, the girl said her mother buys the cookies because she doesn't want to go without them.

"Now we have a problem," Rudd says. "The daughter wants to do the right thing, but mom is not disciplined herself. It's hard to say no to that stuff, and mom doesn't buy fresh fruits and vegetables because they spoil fast."

According to Gallagher, if spoilage weren't an issue, if that mother could get to a grocery store two or three times a week without making an odyssey out of her neighborhood, the family could muster the willpower to make better choices.

"You can't choose healthy food if you don't have access to it," Gallagher says.

A key factor in luring grocers to neighborhoods is the presence of similar retail, called "agglomeration." Simply put, like attracts like, Gallagher explains. Competition keeps stores on their toes also, so when a neighborhood has a lone store, the pressure to provide a variety of healthy alternatives can cease to be a priority. She uses a grocery store on Chicago's Near South Side as an example: The store has fixed costs. They might stop selling cilantro to keep costs down. A shopper goes in looking for cilantro. It's not there. She gets mad and drives to a gentrified neighborhood near downtown to find what she wants. The next time she goes to find organic tomatoes. They're not there, either. She's mad again. The upshot: Either the store loses a customer from the neighborhood or the neighbor compromises her food choices. People compromise.

"Children who grow up in these food deserts have everything stacked against them," Gallagher says. "When you grow up high on sugar, to be frank, and low on nutrients, it's hard to pay attention in school, keep up and graduate."

Food deserts render moot anti-obesity and other health messages when patients receive nutritional counseling in clinics and medical centers.

"We don't consider what they're sending patients into when making a diagnosis," said Dr. Damon Arnold. As Illinois' director of public health, Arnold says doctors are guilty of the sin of omission by not factoring community and environment into their diagnoses.

"You're sending them to the store with a picture of a big triangle, but they can't find the stuff on the triangle," says Arnold, referring to the USDA food pyramid.

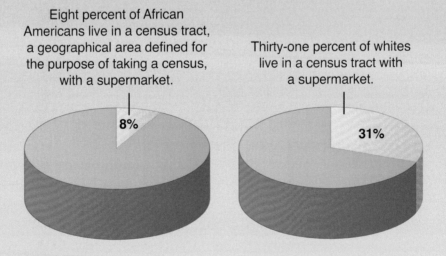

Access to Supermarkets Means Access to Nutritional Food

Eight percent of African Americans live in a census tract, a geographical area defined for the purpose of taking a census, with a supermarket.

8%

Thirty-one percent of whites live in a census tract with a supermarket.

31%

Taken from: "Food Desert Statistics." Teaching Tolerance, a Project of the Southern Poverty Law Center. www.tolerance.org/sites/default/files/general/desert%20stats.pdf.

Communities Need to Take Responsibility

While Congress has been in the throes of hashing out something that can be called health reform, how revolutionary would it be if communities considered food deserts could engage in the ultimate preventive therapy by managing what goes inside their families' bodies?

"Ultimately, cheap food costs more in medical costs," Gallagher says. "It can be measured in the reduction in the quality of life and length of it."

Families, individuals and businesses need incentives to be healthy and to avoid becoming obese in the first place. Researchers agree luring supermarket chains to underserved areas is a talking point but are unsure whether this is the ultimate solution for getting people and healthy food in close proximity. But experts . . . agreed that families on food stamps should be "incentivized" to buy healthy foods by not being allowed to buy empty calories, such as sodas and chips.

Another strategy aimed at reducing children's waistlines is levying high taxes on sodas. The beverage industry has already responded to these efforts by both developing healthier concoctions and vociferously arguing against such taxes. Despite the industry's resistance, the tax approach appeals to John Cawley, an associate professor at Cornell University. An expert on the economics of obesity, he notes how successful cigarette taxes have been in reducing smoking.

Dawn Smith is one 40-year-old mother who won't wait around for the government and university eggheads to realize what she's figured out for herself:

"I'm fat," says Smith.

The necessary cultural shift regarding food and activity is in full effect in Smith's household in suburban Chicago. Where she gave her 13- and 15-year-old daughters hot dogs and chips growing up, she gives yogurt and fruit to her 18-month-old and 6-month-old. Her toddler loves water and has an affinity for healthy foods.

"She loves fruit and things that are good for you," says Smith, an administrative assistant. "Instead of giving them ice cream, I give them yogurt. I've definitely changed in that respect. My older girls grew up in a house where they had family giving them this and that; I never had much control."

Her older daughters, Erica and Taylor, have asked for healthy foods and advice on trimming down. Smith, who grew up thinking families who baked their food were odd, thinks twice when she's preparing meals and makes the necessary substitutions, like bags of salad instead of chips. The teens are also involved in dance, cheerleading, track and other extracurricular activities.

"We're getting to the point where we're steaming vegetables and eating roasted chicken," Smith says. "We're trying to get out of bad habits."

FIVE

Schools Should Make Nutrition Education Part of the Curriculum

Claire Drummond

Claire Drummond is a senior lecturer at Flinders University in Adelaide, Australia. In this viewpoint she asserts the responsibility of schools to teach students about good nutrition. Drummond talks about "food literacy," which refers to the knowledge and skills necessary to select, prepare, and serve food. She says that if students are taught these skills in school, they will be empowered to choose nutritious food. Drummond maintains that nutrition education should be considered an essential life skill and should be part of every curriculum.

A recent television program shown in Australia featured celebrity chef Jamie Oliver asking primary school-aged students in the United States (US) if they recognised a variety of fruits and vegetables.

Holding up a tomato, Jamie Oliver asked the class if they knew what it was—one student answered, [saying] that it was a 'potato'. When Jamie then asked the group if they knew what 'ketchup' was, the same student replied that he knew what ketchup was to which Jamie Oliver replied that ketchup was made from tomatoes. While anecdotal evidence indicates that nutritional knowledge by Australian school students is not as dire, this example of food comprehension from the US raises important questions about the state of nutritional knowledge among school-aged children and whether nutrition education and cooking skills in schools may assist with an increase in nutritional understanding and student empowerment to make healthy food choices.

Poor health among children in the form of obesity and dental caries [tooth decay] is prevalent in Australia; therefore it is essential that good eating habits are established at a young age, so they can be carried into adulthood. Schools offer the ideal place where children and adolescents can be informed of the relevant nutrition education and cooking skills in relation to healthy eating.

Schools provide the most effective and efficient way to reach a large section of the population, including children, school staff and the wider community. Eating behaviours learnt at school may play a significant role in ensuring that 'health enhancing' eating behaviour is practiced into adulthood. While young children progressively acquire and learn eating habits and practices from their family, during their school years the social environment of children diversifies, which in turn influences their food choices. Once a child reaches adolescence, the family becomes less influential and friends, peers and social models are the key influences on eating practices.

Good nutrition during childhood contributes to the maintenance of optimal health and learning capacities. Educational strategies in schools can include efforts to increase health awareness and when taught correctly, teach the skills and knowledge required to improve or strengthen healthy eating habits.

Using a whole school approach to nutrition education, children and adolescents are given the skills to enhance their competence as informed consumers and are able to perform their food choices in a complex society. Evidence also suggests that when a whole school environment approach to health is used, there is a positive impact on aspects of mental and social wellbeing, including self-esteem and bullying. Investigations into the benefits of school-based nutrition programs and subsequent healthy school programs show that the academic performance and mental

ability of students with good nutritional status are significantly higher than those of pupils with poor nutritional status. Given the importance of nutrition education it should be part of the curriculum for all students in primary and secondary schools.

Food Literacy Is an Important Skill

While a relatively new term, the phrase 'food literacy' indicates how we, as individuals and as a community, know and understand food and the skills we need to influence food choice. The term further describes the knowledge, skills and capacities to grow, select, store, prepare, cook and serve food.

Within Australia, there is concern over the disappearance of cooking skills among young people. A lack of role-modeling by parents preparing fresh food and reliance on ready-prepared products could be the reasons for the demise in cooking skills and may lead to food refusal by the child. Furthermore, although the consumption of food around a household table has traditionally been seen as a social occasion amongst family members, research now shows that there is a shift in conventional family mealtime activities due to a variety of reasons (time constraints on the family, two parents working, after school activities, for example). Families are now more likely to 'eat while multitasking', such as consuming food while watching television.

Nutrition education in conjunction with food literacy is an important part of any school curricula. It should aim to provide students with the required knowledge and skills, support self-efficacy as well as encouraging behaviour consistent with a healthy diet. Within the school, however, the challenge for nutrition education lies with bridging the gap between dietary awareness and positive food choice. Children and adolescents are taught by example, in conjunction with nutrition education that occurs in schools. This can be extremely difficult when the school canteen [cafeteria] does not offer healthy options. A conflict of interest may exist then with the accurate and consistent health information provided to the students and the poor nutritional choices available in the school canteen.

Students Should Learn to Make Their Own Food Choices

The aim of school-based health promotion is three-fold: to educate by providing information on nutritional needs; to empower students by increasing recognition of and ability to choose nutritious foods; and to enhance life skills by teaching simple meal preparation and introducing cooking lessons. [M.] Caraher and colleagues contend that without these cooking skills, the empowerment that health educators promote does not exist. In order for students to make correct food choices in the future, they need to be provided with the basic cooking skills in school while still young enough. Nutrition teaching, in conjunction with the provision of food skills in the school setting, has the capacity to empower students to make healthy individual choices, but the schools themselves can become advocates for addressing food security and sustainability. The benefits of promoting healthy food choices at school may transfer to eating patterns outside of school and influence attitudes of the children, their parents and the wider community. The success of nutrition and cooking classes in schools can challenge the traditional model of intergen-

The challenge for nutrition education in school lies with bridging the gap between students' dietary awareness and their making positive food choices.

erational health where students, rather than their parents, can be ones leading healthy change in the family.

If schools use an 'empowerment approach' to educate students on engaging in health promotion behaviors, they are more likely to make changes to their diet. For example, when students are involved in the aspects of their own nutrition education design they have a greater number of successful changes than those students who undertake a more 'traditional' approach. Student centered approaches, teamwork and collaboration are all part of an empowerment approach to nutrition education and allow the student to control their learning and the actions in relation to their health. This notion is supported by current research by [S. Fordyce-Voorham], who recommends that young people should be supported in schools to select and cook their own recipes which can also accommodate vegetarian and other food preferences that students may have.

If students are to make informed choices about their diet and health, they need [to] be provided with the necessary skills about food and nutrition. Improving a student's food literacy, in conjunction with incorporating cooking skills with nutrition education in the school environment, will empower students to take control over what they eat and allow them to make informed choices. Nutrition education and food literacy should therefore be framed as an essential life skill, and schools remain one of the best avenues for disseminating those skills. As schools already deliver a crowded curriculum, teachers must be given support to implement nutrition education and cooking skills into their lesson plans.

SIX

Childhood Obesity Is Caused by Several Factors

Katti Gray

In this viewpoint journalist Katti Gray discusses some of the many facets of the obesity epidemic. She highlights significant factors that contribute to obesity, including race, genetics, class, income level, culture, and nutritional mindsets. She also discusses a University of Tennessee program that helps teach youth about obesity, with hopes that such knowledge will help prevent obesity in the future.

As thousands of brainiac kids from around the globe began descending on the University of Tennessee [UT] for a week of Destination ImagiNation's creative problem-solving summer camp, researchers in health and nutrition on the Knoxville campus couldn't help noticing that scarcely any overly plump children were in that bunch of campers.

On average, they were less sedentary than their peers elsewhere. "And leaner than the kinds of kids you see going to Wal-Mart, especially in Tennessee, where the obesity rate is extremely high," says Dr. Naima Moustaid-Moussa, co-director of UT's multidisciplinary Obesity Research Center, one of several campuses with obesity projects associated with and partially financed by the National Institutes of Health.

As UT launches an afterschool program modeled after Destination ImagiNation in 17 Tennessee counties, UT researchers are banking on the notion that kids who are engaged in thought, ideas and creativity also will become more mindful of nutrition as a fundamental aspect of their daily well-being. The youths will be assigned tasks similar to those undertaken during Destination ImagiNation, which, for example, had youths constructing houses—using only newspapers and tape—large enough to fit a person inside.

"We want them to look at resources they have to solve complex problems," says Dr. Betty Greer, a human ecology professor who helps oversee the summer camp and the pilot anti-obesity project targeting Tennessee's youth. "We're hoping this will make young people more tuned in to eating healthy. When people are more active, their metabolism works better and that hormone that controls hunger is better regulated."

Two-Thirds of Americans Are Overweight or Obese

With Americans fatter and more malnourished than ever—almost two-thirds of the population is considered overweight or obese compared with 56 percent in the late 1980s and early '90s, and people of color and the poor are the most obese of all—federal and university researchers and outreach workers from various anti-obesity organizations aim to make the public more mindful about its food consumption and economic toll of being too big. Some 300,000 deaths per year can be attributed to obesity, and medical costs associated with obesity are estimated at $147 billion annually.

First lady Michelle Obama has been shining a spotlight on childhood obesity and the risks of obese children becoming obese adults, and the health care reform law contains several provisions to fight obesity. For its part, UT is [as of October 2010] halfway through a four-year study of childhood obesity and last month began working with youth in 17 Tennessee counties. Tennessee leapt from fourth place in 2009 to second place this year in a Trust

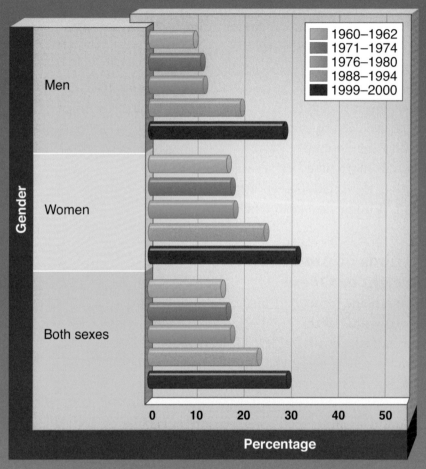

Trends in American Obesity Over Time

These figures, provided by the Centers for Disease Control and Prevention's National Center for Health Statistics, define obesity as a body mass index (BMI) of thirty or above and apply to adults, ages twenty to seventy-four.

Legend:
- 1960–1962
- 1971–1974
- 1976–1980
- 1988–1994
- 1999–2000

Gender: Men, Women, Both sexes

Percentage: 0, 10, 20, 30, 40, 50

Taken from: Centers for Disease Control and Prevention, National Health and Nutrition Examination Survey.

for America's Health–Robert Wood Johnson Foundation ranking of states with the fattest people.

Researchers are also busy investigating the numerous nuances associated with obesity—a chronic disease shaded by class, race, food cultures, nutritional mindsets and household income.

"People with higher incomes can afford health clubs, bicycles, personal trainers, fresh fruits and vegetables and salmon, whereas people who are low-income may live in a food desert where there are few options for healthy food, little exercise equipment, few gyms," says Dr. David Bassett, the UT obesity center's other co-director. "They may not even feel safe walking the streets of the neighborhood. These are some of the discussions we have around here, the ideas that we bounce around. Some of them are proven and some are not. We'd like to believe there are simple answers, but we have to tease apart these questions of race, education and income."

Physiology and Genetics Play a Part in Obesity

There are other important variables, including differences in physiology and genetics. Heeding that reality, the body-mass index (BMI)—a nonclinical calculation of body fat—for normally weighted adults of Asian descent was set by the Centers for Disease Control [and Prevention] at 22.9, which compares with 24.9 for most others. Muscular density, which can vary among and within ethnic groups, is also taken into account, a significant change from yesteryear when appropriate body weight was assessed by a one-size-fits-all standard.

"Five to 7 percent of obesity cases are strictly due to genetic causes," says Moustaid-Moussa, whose research on healthy omega-3 fatty foods will be published later this year [2010] in the *Journal of Nutrition*. "Obesity is a very complex question. That you can be predisposed to being overweight is one aspect of this. On top of that, there is your environment, the matter of food availability, the predisposition of many Hispanics and African-Americans to high blood pressure, high cholesterol. . . ."

Blacks and Latinos have had persistently higher rates of obesity than any ethnic group. Black women are at the top in that hierarchy, with roughly 50 percent of them identified as overweight (a BMI higher than 25, generally speaking) or obese (BMI of 30 or higher). That compares with roughly a third of White women, according to the latest available data from the Centers for Disease Control, National Center for Health Statistics and National Health and Nutrition Examination Survey. Other snapshots of their data show that all poor women (those living at or below 130 percent of the official poverty rate) are twice as likely to be obese than women with higher incomes. Starting out, low-income Black and White girls generally have similar BMIs but that gap widens by the time they turn 19, with Black females becoming weightier.

Income is not a statistically significant factor among men, with obesity rates remaining fairly equal across racial and ethnic groups. However, Mexican-American men are more overweight and obese than non-Latino Whites or Blacks, and non-Latino White males are slightly more overweight or obese than Black men, partly because employed Black men are more likely to be laborers, burning off the calories. Household economics also is less of a factor in whether young children are overweight, except among non-Latino White youths from poor families who tend to be fatter than youths from higher-income clans of other races.

Increases in Type 2 Diabetes Drive the Discussion on Obesity

Rising diagnoses of obesity-linked Type 2 diabetes, one among several fat-related diseases, in young people is helping to drive the focus on obesity. Type 2 diabetes used to primarily afflict adults. "We're aiming to enhance the self-management of people with diabetes, promoting healthier eating and what that means," says nutritionist Robin Nwankwo, a diabetes educator at the University of Michigan's Diabetes Research and Training Center in Detroit. "And we're constantly challenged to provide that information to people with so many other factors at play: long-standing eating habits, the belief that they've no time to prepare food from scratch, limited access to food in the areas of Detroit and Toledo (Ohio) that we serve. Those barriers and personal preferences conflict strongly with what we're trying to achieve."

Spreading the word on what it takes to keep weight in check, and understand caloric intake and food ingredients that help or

There are numerous factors associated with obesity, including social class, race, nutritional mindsets, ethnic food cultures, and household income.

hinder the body is the goal of projects like the one UT is piloting for Tennessee's youth. It also is the aim of outreach programs such as UT Extension's online tutorials on grocery shopping, nutrition, cooking and the like, and of courses offered to UT students.

University of Tennessee Students Learn About Obesity

Dr. Guoxun Chen's undergraduate course on understanding obesity averages about a dozen enrollees at a time; 28,000 students are on the Knoxville campus, the UT system's flagship. "I try to get them to understand the genetic and environmental aspects of this," says Chen. "I also talk about traditions of food and metabolic processes," including the rapid-fire absorption of processed foods and how, say, whole grain bread is better than highly processed, high-fructose white bread because the body works harder to digest and absorb whole grains.

Those are not surprising facts, given the history of food production and consumption. For example, Chen says, Arizona's Pima Indians were lean until around 1890 when natural environmental shifts caused their crop irrigation systems to dry up.

"The United States government began subsidizing food, providing food for them. They became a population with high rates of diabetes and obesity," Chen says, adding, however, that a contingent of Pima moved into the mountains of Mexico and kept farming. "Even today, their current rates of obesity are far lower than their American cousins. Our genes have evolved to let us be obese wherever food is abundant and there is a lack of physical activity. It's takes a little bit of work to eat well."

Government spending priorities haven't helped promote physical activity needed to combat obesity. For example, just 2 percent of federal spending on transportation goes toward biking and walking trails, says Bassett. His survey of Ontario, Canada's agrarian Amish, who maintain a proverbial meat-and-potato diet, consuming large portions and often chasing that with dessert, also found that community to be almost obesity-free. Its men take 18,000 steps per day and women 15,000, Bassett says. That's three times the amount walked by the average U.S. resident.

Says Bassett: "I've been in this field for 22 years and I vacillate between hopefulness and discouragement. I grew up in a sort of different world, walking to elementary, middle school and high school. My parents had a vegetable garden. We never watched more than 30 minutes of television a day."

Not so now. Half of all Black kids spend more than three hours a day in front of the tube. Blacks watch more television than any other group. And research has linked passive television watching—as opposed to play or other activity—directly to obesity.

Says Nwankwo of her hopes for the future: "We are starting to see and hear more younger adults, people in their 20s, early 30s, starting to make the connection between illness and obesity and recognizing that this is a problem. They're being pulled into care-giving and they simply do not want that."

SEVEN

Michelle Obama's Let's Move! Program Is Wasteful and Intrusive

Michael Tennant

In the following viewpoint journalist Michael Tennant discusses First Lady Michelle Obama's Let's Move! program. Tennant states that helping children grow up to be a healthy weight is a worthy goal, but he opposes excessive government spending to help achieve this goal. He believes that such actions as eliminating "food desserts" and regulating school lunches do not improve nutrition and are a waste of federal money.

ObamaCare makes every American's health the government's business, but [President] Barack Obama is not the only member of his family interested in employing the federal government as our national nanny. His wife, Michelle Obama, is equally concerned with using her own bully pulpit and her husband's power as a means of whipping Americans into shape—for our own good, of course.

Mrs. Obama's "Let's Move!" campaign has as its stated objective to "solve the challenge of childhood obesity within a generation so that children born today will reach adulthood at a healthy weight." This is indeed a worthy goal; no one wants kids to grow up overweight and ill.

However, Obama's method of addressing this issue consists of an array of Washington-issued mandates, government-corporate collusion, federal spending, and, most disturbingly, the use of government schools as food police. This would be unsettling enough if she were just some think-tank guru spouting off a wish list; but since she is married to the President of the United States, it is within her reach actually to impose her agenda—and much of it is already in progress.

Large Grocery Stores Do Not Help Healthy Eating

Among the in-progress initiatives in Obama's agenda is the Healthy Food Financing Initiative, the purpose of which is to eliminate so-called "food deserts," defined on the "Let's Move!" website as "low-income urban and rural neighborhoods that are more than a mile from a supermarket." The idea is that the lack of a large grocery store limits a community's food choices, often forcing them to shop at convenience stores and other small retailers who offer few fresh fruits and vegetables but plenty of processed, unhealthful foods.

The Healthy Food Financing Initiative is, according to the website, "a partnership between the U.S. Departments of Treasury, Agriculture, and Health and Human Services to invest $400 million a year to provide innovative financing to develop healthy food retailers to underserved areas and help places such as convenience stores and bodegas carry healthier food options." How generous of them to "invest" hundreds of millions of other people's dollars!

Obama has named the Pennsylvania Fresh Food Initiative, a Keystone State program that combines public and private funding to provide grants and low-cost loans to grocers that operate in low-income areas, as an example of what the federal program should look like.

There is little evidence that Pennsylvania's program and other similar initiatives have any significant effects on produce con-

A student competes in a shopping cart relay during an event sponsored by First Lady Michelle Obama's Let's Move! antiobesity campaign, which critics claim wastes money and intrudes on privacy.

sumption and obesity rates. Noting that several studies have documented a link between easy access to healthful foods and both better eating habits and decreased obesity, David C. Holzman wrote in an article for *Environmental Health Perspectives*:

However, the actual health toll from living in a food desert environment has not been tabulated in a peer-reviewed study. Moreover, the only 2 studies that examined diets before and after grocery stores were installed in food deserts—rather than comparing neighborhoods with grocery stores to similar neighborhoods without—are not encouraging, says Steven Haider, an associate professor of economics at Michigan State University. Neil Wrigley et al. wrote in volume 35, issue 1 (2003) of *Built Environment* that people consumed an extra half a serving of fruit and/or vegetables daily, while Steve Cummins et al. reported no change in the Winter 2005 issue of *Planning Healthy Towns and Cities*. And global nutrition professor Barry Popkin of the University of North Carolina at Chapel Hill says a January 2009 workshop he chaired at the Institute of Medicine on the public health effects of food deserts "could find no evidence that adding new retail stores to depressed areas changed what people consumed."

In other words, the Healthy Food Financing Initiative is nothing more than a feel-good program that uses taxpayers' money to help politically favored businesses locate in areas that are otherwise unsuitable for their operations. As with most public-private partnerships, profits will be privatized and losses socialized. . . .

Teaming Up with Private Corporations

In her web chat Obama said, "Kids are malleable, and they're also open to learn." With that in mind, she is seeing to it that her message is communicated to them in a variety of ways.

For example, she said, "We want to see every major sports league in this country finding a way to invest in the health of our kids. I want to see every athlete, every Olympian in a school." To that end, she appeared at a baseball clinic at the home of the Baltimore Orioles and "announced that [Major League Baseball (MLB)] and the MLB Players Association will team with the White House in the Let's Move campaign," according to a July 20 [2010] Associated Press report. Thirty ballplayers have agreed to appear in public service announcements for Obama's initiative. The New York Mets have already sent players to local schools, where, according to a press release, "players joined students in fitness programs in support of First Lady Michelle Obama's Let's Move campaign to combat childhood obesity through exercise and nutrition."

Another of Obama's means of getting the word out is through television shows with juvenile audiences. "I hope that we're seeing more marketing of healthy foods to our kids so that we start seeing some of our partners like Disney and others taking a step and ensuring that we're having conversations with our kids in the venues that they love best, those Disney shows, and we're talking about nutrition," Obama said in her web chat.

Disney has, in fact, already gotten on board, using its media juggernaut to spread Obama's message. A February 9 [2010] Disney press release explained:

Disney will create a series of PSAs [public service announcements] featuring the First Lady and leading Disney Channel stars to inspire healthier eating habits, physical activity and more. The messages will be featured across Disney's kid and family targeted media platforms, including Disney Channel, Disney XD, Radio Disney, and Disney.com and will begin airing later this year. . . .

At least one episode of each [Disney Channel] series currently in production—including "Hannah Montana," "Wizards of Waverly Place," "Sonny With a Chance," "Zeke and Luther," "Phineas and Ferb" and "The Suite Life on Deck"—centers on a healthy lifestyle theme. In addition, over 100 interstitials [short programs] have been dedicated to encouraging healthier lifestyles. They include "Pass the Plate," a global effort to both inform and empower viewers, showing them how kids just like them around the world enjoy and benefit from healthy foods, and "Get'cha Head in the Game," an interstitial series that inspires kids to follow their dreams through physical activity.

This is not just a few harmless PSAs to show that the company supposedly cares about its audience; it's a major media campaign requiring a great deal of trouble and expense. Even if it does center solely on nutrition and fitness, it shows the lengths to which big media corporations will go to indoctrinate kids with the government's message, especially if they think there's good publicity in it for them. What might Disney, Major League Baseball,

The Food Pyramid Becomes "My Plate"

In June 2011 the US Department of Agriculture (USDA) introduced "My Plate," a new graphic to represent the proportions of a balanced meal. Some commentators have criticized the government for letting special interest groups unduly influence USDA recommendations.

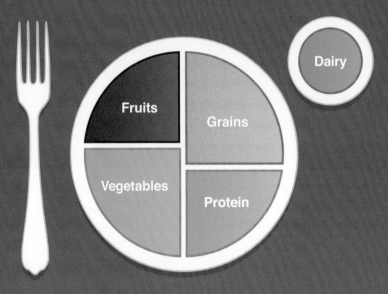

Taken from: US Department of Agriculture. www.choosemyplate.gov.

and other corporate entities with great influence over children do to promote other government priorities, even those explicitly opposed by those same children's parents? Vigilance is required.

Governmental Nutritional Advice Is Not Valid

Furthermore, how valid is the nutritional advice the government has to offer anyway? Federal nutritional standards have always been subject to political pressure. [Jim] Powell [author of *Bully Boy: The Truth About Theodore Roosevelt's Legacy*] mentions that [Harvey Washington] Wiley [chief chemist for the Bureau of Chemistry]—who, again, had a vested interest in seeing the sugar industry prosper—"encouraged Americans to consume more sugar. . . . 'Childhood without candy,' he remarked, 'would be Heaven without harps.'"

The USDA [US Department of Agriculture] Food Pyramid, too, is hardly immune to politics. The *Wall Street Journal* described the lobbying that took place when the USDA's dietary guidelines came up for their pentennial [five-year] review in 2002—"an exercise," said the *Journal*, "that attracts not only critics from the world of medicine but industry lobbyists and those promoting the virtues of various food groups and diets."

Some medical researchers criticized the pyramid's emphasis on grains at the expense of fruits and vegetables, possibly due to the influence of the grain lobby. Others complained that the pyramid was either too critical of fats or failed to indicate that dairy products—dairy farmers have a powerful lobby, too—should be consumed in low-fat varieties.

Meanwhile, wrote the *Journal*, "During the last revision, the advisory committee considered changing the 1995 recommendation of adhering to a diet 'moderate' in salt and sugar to 'eating less salt and sugar.' The powerful sugar industry fought the change, and the guidelines now tell consumers to 'moderate your intake of sugars.' (The 'less salt' revision stuck.)" A 2004 *Journal* article explained how lobbyists worked to keep sugar, potatoes, and bread in the pyramid before the next revision.

The current version of the pyramid has also been criticized for its seeming genuflections to special interests, such as the prominence of dairy products, which are not necessarily essential to a healthy diet (as the health of many of those who abstain from dairy products attests).

Thus, even if one trusts media conglomerates not to fill young skulls full of mush with more controversial government propaganda, it still remains the case that telling kids to follow the feds' nutritional advice could be hazardous to their health.

School Nutrition Policies Have Been Ineffective

Obama's primary avenue for fighting childhood obesity is clearly the public schools. The "Let's Move!" website emphasizes them greatly, and Obama did so as well in her web chat. Asked what progress toward her goal she envisioned in the next five years, Obama said,

> In five years I hope to see us making progress in our school lunches. I hope that we have a viable and well-funded school nutrition act, child nutrition act, and that we're seeing the quality go up in our schools, we're seeing more education going on around nutrition in our schools. We want to see more schools participating in community gardens and being the place where kids are gonna get their first taste of fresh fruit and vegetables and understand how that grows.

The child nutrition reauthorization act of which Obama speaks was passed by the House Education and Labor Committee on July 15 [2010], an act for which Agriculture Secretary Tom Vilsack effusively praised the committee on the "Let's Move!" website. The act, if passed, will require more nutrition education in schools and force all food sold in schools, whether in the regular cafeteria line, in vending machines, a la carte, or even in school fundraisers, to meet federal nutrition standards.

Of course, as we have already seen, those standards are somewhat less than scientific. But even supposing they are scientifically accurate, the policy will amount to denying kids various foods that Washington bureaucrats deem unhealthful, regardless of the health and weight of the individual child or the wishes of his parents.

One would hope that such a policy, onerous and unconstitutional though it is, would at least have the beneficial effect of reducing obesity and improving health among children. However, existing school nutrition programs premised on the same theory have been less than rousing successes, as Harriet Brown reported in a 2006 *New York Times* article, "Well-Intentioned Food Police May Create Havoc With Children's Diets":

> Like other misguided public health campaigns . . . , putting children on de facto diets at school just doesn't work. In a 2003 experiment involving 41 schools, more than 1,700

children—many of them American Indian—were served lower-calorie and lower-fat lunches and were taught about healthy eating and lifestyles.

While the children took in fewer calories from fat at school, they experienced no significant reduction in their percentage of body fat.

Another study, in rural Nebraska in the mid-1990s, put one group of elementary school students on lower-fat and lower-sodium lunches, increased their physical activity at school and offered more education about nutrition. Compared with students having no special program, the active, lower-fat group showed no differences in body weight or fat, or in levels of total cholesterol, insulin or glucose after two years.

Researchers concluded that pupils whose school lunches offered 25 percent fat (compared with 31 percent in the control group) were compensating for the reduction by eating higher-fat foods at home.

The act praised by Vilsack and Obama, officially the Improving Nutrition for America's Children Act, also expands the federal school lunch program to weekends, holidays, and summer vacations, thus ensuring that taxpayers get soaked even more and that the recipients of these "free" lunches grow up to be grateful wards of the state, disinclined to raise a ruckus about its steady encroachments upon their liberties. . . .

The "Let's Move!" Recommendations Are Intrusive and Wasteful

The "Let's Move!" website offers many other detailed anti-obesity suggestions for parents, schools, mayors and local officials, community leaders, chefs, and kids. These recommendations run the gamut from the relatively innocuous (asking parents to provide fruit for their children's snacks and telling kids to do jumping jacks) to the highly intrusive (setting "goals for improving healthy behaviors among [school] staff"). Then there are standard big-government solutions, such as asking local officials to encourage families to get their kids into the government's school lunch program and to offer "free" (i.e., taxpayer-funded) intramural sports. The First Nanny even tells churches to "provide healthy selections" and reduce portion sizes at congregational dinners!

Mrs. Obama's anti-childhood-obesity campaign is far from the usual first lady fluff. It has serious implications for constitutional government, individual privacy, and family stability, especially when combined with other intrusive federal programs such as ObamaCare. With the federal government already morbidly obese, it is no time to be packing on another ton of unconstitutional, wasteful, intrusive, and probably counterproductive programs. Instead, let's move to trim this fat from Uncle Sam's waistline faster than you can say Jenny Craig.

EIGHT

Exercise Seen as Priming the Pump for Students

Debra Viadero

Debra Viadero is an editor for *Education Week* magazine. In this viewpoint she discusses several studies that indicate that exercise can help students' academic performance. She says that since the No Child Left Behind Act of 2001, schools have been reducing or eliminating physical education and recess, which may be a mistake. Among the studies she mentions, one concluded that students who exercised twice as long increased their academic performance by twice as much; another determined that exercise immediately before class was more helpful than if exercise and classes were separated by several hours.

At 7:45 a.m. each weekday, while most of his peers at Naperville Central High School in Naperville, Ill., are sitting in class and groggy with sleep, 15-year-old Matt Bray is running sprints, jumping rope, lifting weights, and engaging in other activities, all aimed at getting his heart pumping.

This early-morning exercise class is about more than getting in shape, though. A small but growing number of experts and educators suggest that Mr. Bray is priming his brain for learning at the same time he's sculpting his biceps.

Debra Viadero, "Exercise Seen as Priming Pump for Students' Academic Strides," *Education Week*, February 13, 2008, pp. 14–15. Copyright © 2008 by Editorial Projects in Education. All rights reserved. Reproduced by permission.

"It's been actually raising my grades a little bit higher," Mr. Bray, a freshman, said of the class, which he has been taking since September "Now I'm getting A's and B's on average," he said. "In junior high, I was getting B's and C's."

Seven or eight years ago, studies offered mixed results on the question of whether exercise can boost brain function in children and adolescents. Experts are beginning to contend, however, that the case is getting stronger.

"There's sort of no question about it now," said Dr. John J. Ratey, a clinical associate professor of psychiatry at Harvard Medical School. "The exercise itself doesn't make you smarter, but it puts the brain of the learners in the optimal position for them to learn."

Range of Benefits

Dr. Ratey is the author of *Spark: The Revolutionary New Science of Education and the Brain*, a book published last month by Little, Brown and Co. It draws together emerging findings from neuroscientific, biomedical, and educational research that correlate exercise with a wide range of brain-related benefits—improving attention, reducing stress and anxiety, and staving off cognitive decline in old age, for example.

The interest in documenting a link between exercise and learning in children and adolescents comes as trends in physical activity seem to point in the opposite direction. Studies suggest that, with 30 percent of the nation's schoolchildren classified as overweight, childhood obesity is reaching epidemic proportions.

Proponents of the educational benefits of exercise maintain that the federal No Child Left Behind Act, which puts pressure on schools to raise students' test scores in core academic subjects, is prompting some schools to cut back on time for physical education classes and recess. Nationwide, Dr. Ratey writes in his book, only 6 percent of schools now offer PE five days a week. "At the same time," he adds, "kids are spending 5.5 hours a day in front of a screen of some sort—television, computer, or handheld device."

"Had the creators of No Child Left Behind looked at the data, they would've realized that physical activity is good for the brain," said Charles H. Hillman, an associate professor of kinesiology at the University of Illinois at Urbana-Champaign.

With his university colleague Darla M. Castelli, Mr. Hillman assessed the physical-fitness levels of 239 3rd and 5th graders from four Illinois elementary schools. Their findings, published last year in the *Journal of Sport & Exercise Psychology*, show that children who got good marks on two measures of physical fitness—those that gauge aerobic fitness and body-mass index—tended also to have higher scores on state exams in reading and mathematics. That relationship also held true regardless of children's gender or socioeconomic differences.

Bowled Over

Another study published last year, involving 163 overweight children in Augusta, Ga., found, in addition, that the cognitive and academic benefits of exercise seemed to increase with the size of the dose.

For that study, a cross-disciplinary research team randomly assigned children to one of three groups. One group received 20 minutes of physical activity every day after school. Another group got a 40-minute daily workout, and the third group got no special exercise sessions.

After 14 weeks, the children who made the greatest improvement, as measured by both a standardized academic test and a test that measured their level of executive function—thinking processes, in other words, that involve planning, organizing, abstract thought, or self-control—were those who spent 40 minutes a day playing tag and taking part in other active games designed by the researchers. The cognitive and academic gains for the 20-minutes-a-day group were half as large.

"I was frankly bowled over by the results," said Catherine L. Davis, the lead author of the study, a preliminary version of which was published in December in *Research Quarterly for Exercise and Sport*. "It's like a staircase, which is considered strong evidence for causation," added Ms. Davis, who is an associate professor of pediatrics at the Medical College of Georgia in Augusta.

PE Experiment

In the meantime, educators in Naperville District 203, a suburban district of 18,600 students just west of Chicago, have been conducting some informal experiments on their own. With advice from Dr. Ratey, the school instituted what is now called a "learning readiness" PE class where students such as Mr. Bray can choose from more than a dozen heart-pumping activities.

The students wear heart monitors, which they check to maintain a heart rate of 160 to 190 beats a minute for 25-minute stretches at a time throughout the week.

When the class started in the fall of 2004, it included about a dozen students who were targeted for extra help based on low test

Exercise and the Brain

These images show an average composite of twenty student brains taking the same test.

Brains after sitting quietly   **Brains after twenty-minute walk**

Taken from: Paul Zientarski. "Learning Is a Moving Experience." www.fitness.gov/about-us/council-meetings/council-meeting-2011/learning-is-a-moving-experience.pdf.

scores in reading and teacher recommendations. Reading teachers were also recruited to infuse a bit of literacy instruction into some of the activities.

One game called for students to race around on scooters to match words with their definitions written on pieces of paper on the floor, said Paul Zientarski, the school's instructional coordinator for physical education and health.

After their early-morning PE session, the students joined other struggling readers and writers in a special literacy class designed to give them extra academic help in those areas.

At the end of one semester, Naperville educators found, students who took part in both the early-morning exercise program and the literacy class showed 1.34 of a year's growth on standardized reading tests, according to Mr. Zientarski. The gain for the students in the literacy-only group, in comparison, was seven-tenths of a year.

Naperville educators tried the same approach the following school year with an introductory algebra class for students having difficulty in mathematics and saw even more dramatic gains. Students who both exercised and took the extra-help math class increased their scores on a standardized algebra test by 20.4 percent. The gain for students in the control group was 3.87 percent, according to Mr. Zientarski.

The school did not get the same results, though, a year later when the "learning readiness" classes and the literacy classes were scheduled six hours apart.

Students who had literacy lessons right after exercising did just as well, but improvements were smaller for students with afternoon literacy classes. That led Naperville Central's guidance counselors to recommend that all students schedule their toughest academic classes right after PE.

"We now have three years of data showing what we have, and we really think we're on to something," Mr. Zientarski added.

But district administrators would like to enlist university-based researchers to do more-formal studies before incorporating major scheduling changes districtwide.

"We have so many different variables that could affect how we evaluate the course," said Jody Wirt, the district's associate superintendent for instruction. "Is it the class size? Or the teachers?"

Mental "Miracle Gro"

Likewise, scientists are still not entirely sure how exercise primes the brain for learning. But, according to Dr. Ratey, they have some good ideas.

Laboratory studies in mice and humans, for instance, show that exercise prompts the brain to produce greater amounts of a protein called brain-derived neurotrophic factor or BDNF, which Dr. Ratey likes to call "Miracle-Gro" for the brain.

It encourages brain cells to sprout synapses, which are crucial to forming the connections the brain needs to make in order to learn. It also strengthens cells and protects them from dying out.

Other research also suggests that exercise plays a role in neurogenesis, the production of new brain cells, in middle-aged and older adults and in laboratory animals.

"There's no way to say for sure that exercise improves learning capacity for kids, but it certainly seems to correlate to that," Dr. Ratey said. What seems to continue to be important, though, is what gets put in those brain cells—in other words, whether students are given complex learning fodder to practice and master.

It's also not likely, Dr. Ratey said, that just any physical education curriculum will produce the kinds of benefits that Naperville saw with its "learning readiness" classes.

At the instigation of former physical education teacher Phil Lawler, the Naperville district has been at the forefront of a national movement for the "new PE," a philosophy that promotes teaching students how to be fit and lead healthy lives, rather than focusing on sports skills and game rules.

"No more getting picked last for basketball. No more climbing ropes or playing dodgeball," said Mr. Lawler, who now works for a Kansas City, Mo.–based foundation, called PE4Life, that trains teachers and promotes the concept nationwide.

A teacher leads a physical education class. Recent studies have found that physical activity can lead to higher academic achievement.

Mr. Lawler and Mr. Zientarski, for instance, began using heart-rate monitors with all their classes more than a decade ago.

They also raised money to install climbing walls and ropes courses in their schools and brought in kayaks and sophisticated exercise equipment that incorporates video games and virtual-reality technology to make exercise more engaging for students.

Traditional sports are still taught, but the games, such as three-on-three basketball, take place in smaller groups, Mr. Lawler said. "This isn't just a few PE teachers with a wild idea anymore," he said. "It's combining what should go on in a quality physical education program with some of the highest-quality research in the world in neuroscience and cognitive science."

NINE

Alternative Sports Can Help Improve Physical Education

Ron Schachter

In this viewpoint journalist Ron Schachter discusses a recent trend toward teaching nontraditional activities in physical education classes rather than team sports. He says that students who learn activities such as rock climbing, cycling, hiking, fishing, yoga, and inline skating are likely to continue these activities throughout their life, unlike students who learn team sports such as basketball or football. He acknowledges that these programs can be expensive and urges schools to seek additional funding to support the programs.

When Saul Lerner became director of physical education, athletics and health for the Bellmore-Merrick (N.Y.) School District 14 years ago, football, soccer, basketball and floor hockey were the staples of most physical education classes on Long Island and around the rest of the country. "The emphasis was on sports you would watch on TV. That was the mindset of physical educators," Lerner explains.

But mindset has begun to change—spurred by students' reduced appetite for team-oriented sports, their increased appetite for junk food, and their shifting redefinition of "activity" to mean surfing the Web and running their fingers over the message pads of mobile phones. There don't appear to be any statistics that prove fewer students are interested in team-oriented sports, but anecdotally, physical education and wellness directors indicate that they're seeing more kids drawn to activities other than conventional sports.

"Fewer and fewer kids today are playing sports, and more are obese," Lerner says. "Kids have great thumbs now but can't run three steps."

The fact that our nation's youth are in worse shape now than a generation ago is widely known. A landmark study in 2007 by the U.S. Centers for Disease Control found that almost 17 percent of American children ages 6 to 19 were obese, triple the number from 1980, although a subsequent report released last July found that the percentage of obese youngsters and teens had dipped slightly to just below 15 percent.

Lerner and his district have responded with plenty of steps of their own, turning the conventional definition of phys ed on its head. Nowadays students at Bellmore-Merrick's three high schools and one of the district's middle schools take classes in everything from Pilates to step aerobics, clamber up and down climbing walls, go cycling, and lately have taken to skateboarding in school—activities available as electives to satisfy New York state's weekly two-hour physical education requirement.

Nontraditional Activities Can Last a Lifetime

"There are so many kids today interested in being physically active but not interested in competitive sports, and there's a recognition that our job in physical education is to motivate all kids to be physically active for a lifetime," notes Steve Jeffries, who directs the graduate program in physical education at Central Washington University and serves as president of the National Association for Sport and Physical Education (NASPE). Jeffries is leading by example, having added an outdoor class to the CWU graduate curriculum focused on rock climbing, hiking, inline skating and even juggling. The university has run a physical education Summer Camp for the past 20 years, from which children around Washington state attend.

In addition, when most student athletes leave high school, they don't return to playing team sports elsewhere. "Ninety-seven percent of our athletes will complete their athletics when they graduate high school," adds Chris McCarthy, who created a health club for students at the Katonah-Lewisboro (N.Y.) School District and is a big proponent of alternative sports and fitness.

Of course, students in the Bellmore-Merrick district reporting for physical education class can still choose from an assortment of more traditional sports. But Lerner is hoping that more students choose activities that will last them a lifetime. "An adult basketball league usually requires 20 players and a gym," he points out. "But when it comes to cycling, you can do it when you want to."

Lerner, who played basketball himself in high school, knows from personal experience. "With four kids, it's a constant struggle at my stage of life to say, 'I'm going to play basketball.' I can cycle when they're sleeping. In physical education classes, the winners are the kids who continue to do things."

Jeffries adds that the potential benefits to students' academic performance are large. "There's more and more evidence that working out and staying in shape makes you perform better in other areas," Jeffries suggests.

Among the growing body of research, a 2006 study of fifth-, seventh-, and ninth-grade students in California found that those who had met six fitness criteria—from aerobic capacity to body mass index—scored more than 40 percent higher on standardized math and reading tests than classmates who had met none of the criteria.

Fitness Equipment in Schools Is Beneficial, but Expensive

In Katonah-Lewisboro, McCarthy—in his first year as the district's director of health, physical education, athletics and wellness—aims to replicate the physical education program he had developed over the past decade for high school students in nearby Rye Neck (N.Y.) Union Free School District. "One of the main concepts is creating a health club within a school, in

Kids are encouraged to participate in activities such as rock climbing, cycling, hiking, fishing, and yoga because, unlike taking part in team sports like football and baseball, they have a better chance of continuing these activities through adulthood.

which we educate kids on how to assess what they're doing to meet their goals," he explains.

The elements of that health club include stationary bikes, treadmills and weights, along with circuit training and employing heart monitors to measure students' progress. "We take data of what's actually taking place in their exercise," he says. "It's really training with a purpose," he emphasizes. "At Rye Neck, we went from a scenario of severely limited participation of students in phys ed electives to where the superintendent was so impressed with the level of student participation that he said, 'I don't believe what I'm seeing.'"

But highly affluent Rye Neck can afford such high-tech "clubs" in its schools. The 20 bikes for the spinning class cost close to $1,000 each, and installing an indoor adventure course—consisting of climbing walls and an assortment of beams and other equipment for students to balance on—exceeded $50,000. "Fortunately, I had a lot of support within the district," McCarthy says, noting that in Katonah-Lewisboro his budget is more limited than at Rye Neck. He has turned instead to the high school's booster club to finance the first phase of a weight room, training programs and monitoring equipment, but the spinning and adventure courses will have to wait until he can find a way to secure the necessary funding.

Back in Long Island, Lerner also has found an administration willing and able to support his expansion of alternative physical education, including the addition of skateboarding. It cost thousands for the physical education instructor to train at a skateboarding facility in Boulder, Colo., and more than $100 each for boards that won't scuff the gym floors on which students practice new techniques.

The urban Roanoke (Va.) City Public Schools offers fishing as part of its physical education curriculum. The district has reeled in a $3,225 grant from the Future Fisherman Foundation, which allowed two physical education teachers—from William Fleming and Patrick Henry high schools, football and basketball stalwarts in that part of the state—to take a one-week summer seminar in Michigan on teaching fishing and then take several field trips with their students during the school year to Virginia's ponds and lakes.

Yoga Helps Students Slow Down

In more than 100 public schools in Minnesota, physical education teachers are discovering an ancient ritual to promote lifelong physical activity. These teachers have been certified to teach yoga to elementary, middle and high school students.

For the past three years, Rochelle Patten has begun her biweekly physical education classes at the Susan B. Anthony Middle School in the Minneapolis Public Schools with 20 minutes of yoga instruction. And while Patten says her students are quick to learn that yoga provides a real workout, they are also absorbing some of the more meditative aspects of the practice, including grounding, stillness and listening.

"I just feel that children have a hard time focusing and that they find a lot of anxiety in daily life," much of it generated from high expectations to perform at school, says Patten, who earned her certification through a six-month online course from Yoga Calm, an educational organization based in Portland, Ore.

Although physical education is not required for Minnesota's seventh- and eighth-graders, Patten notes that 400 of her school's 600 students sign up for her classes each year. "My kids have really bought into it," she continues.

Patten says that practicing yoga will pay short- and long-term benefits to those students. "The research has shown that kids who practice yoga or meditation perform better in class," she says, pointing to a 2003 study of yoga classes at the Los Angeles' inner-city Accelerated School, where participating students also raised their GPAs. "But I also hope that later in life they will have the skills to slow things down."

Alternative Physical Education Programs Require Strong Advocates

Lerner says the idea of alternative phys ed activities is no longer revolutionary, and a number of neighboring schools now offer everything from kickboxing to hip-hop dancing. But programs like Bellmore-Merrick's and Rye Neck's are proving more the exception than the rule, in large part because of the price tag. "It's very tough to change a program in a district where your P.E. budget is $1 a kid, especially when you're dependent on equipment and facilities," observes Jeffries. Once started, Jeffries says,

Trends in American Obesity Among Children and Adolescents, 1963–2008

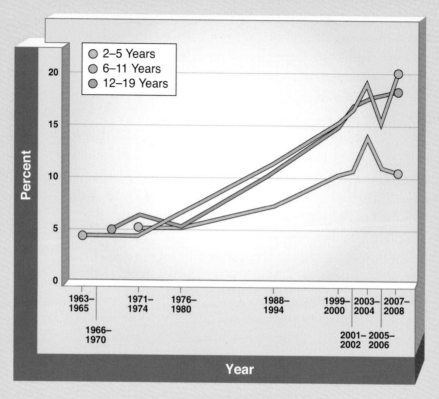

Taken from: Cynthia Ogden and Margaret Carroll. "Prevalence of Obesity Among Children and Adolescents: United States, Trends 1963–1965 Through 2007–2008." National Center for Health Statistics/CDC, 2010.

alternative programs need committed advocates to keep them going.

Besides advocating for alternative physical education, NASPE president Steve Jeffries notes that physical education classes can draw more students into traditional team sports because those with marginal playing abilities get to play in class. "Over the years, there's been too much emphasis on the higher skills," Jeffries admits.

Bane McCracken, the founder of a physical education program that had students at Cabell-Midland High School in the Cabell

County (W.Va.) Schools walk, hike and ride bicycles, still prefers an approach that goes beyond computer-led exercise classes and the traditional playing field. "There are some great programs going on, but there are still a lot of schools that haven't caught on yet," laments McCracken, who is no longer at the district. "There's a big disconnect from what we should be doing and what we are doing."

The greatest hope for the continued growth of such alternatives, McCracken and other proponents agree, lies in changing the prevailing mindset of physical education departments and finding the funding to pay for new programs.

TEN

Technology Can Help Improve Physical Education

Naomi Dillon

Naomi Dillon is a senior editor for *American School Board Journal*. In this viewpoint she considers how technology can be used in physical education classes. She discusses tools that are used to track progress, such as pedometers and heart rate monitors, and also talks about video games such as *Dance Dance Revolution* that make physical fitness fun.

For today's students, technology has made life easier and more exciting. It has created more opportunities for learning. At the same time, the Internet, instant messaging, video games, and cellphones have contributed to a generation that is far less active and more obese than ever.

With health officials predicting a child obesity rate of 20 percent by 2010, the consequences of doing nothing are dire. Kids who are overweight or obese by the age [of] 8 are 80 percent more likely to remain overweight or obese as adults.

So, for schools, the question is how to use the power of technology to drive students toward a healthier lifestyle. From pedometers and heart rate monitors to computerized assessment programs and video exercise games, more and more educators are exploring and turning to technology to improve the health and wellness of their students.

"Right now people appreciate the fact that we have an obesity issue, that there is a relationship between physical activity and cognitive ability," says Bonnie Mohnsen, who operates a California-based online business that provides schools with technology tools to improve physical education programs. "We could have someone incredibly intelligent and well-educated but if they die of coronary heart disease at 25, what good would we be doing as a school system?"

Make It Matter

Mohnsen's career began well before educators thought about using technology to stimulate learning. A former P.E. teacher, she has witnessed the evolution that now incorporates technology as a viable teaching instrument.

"Historically, the first use of technology in physical education was for fitness reporting," Mohnsen says. "So you would assess students, input the data, and print out a report."

Data collection has long been one of the most popular uses of technology among physical education teachers. By and large, the process is essentially the same, but the equipment has become more sophisticated, the criterion for the data has changed, and the results are viewed and developed by more than just teachers.

"In the old days, almost everybody used the Presidential [Fitness Test]," says Phil Lawler, director of instruction and outreach for the child fitness advocacy group PE4life. "So they used to compare everybody to everybody in class. If you were an athlete, great, but there wasn't a lot of incentive if you weren't."

Helping Students Achieve Good Health

Today, Lawler uses software programs and systems like the FITNESSGRAM and Tri Fit to gather and track extensive data. Standards are based on good health, not athletic ability.

"When our seniors graduate, they get a 25-page printout of their health profile going all the way back to the fourth grade," says Lawler, who directs a PE4life training facility at a suburban Chicago middle school. "Hydration level, blood pressure, family history, nutrition analysis, cholesterol screening. We definitely saved some young people."

Conversely, it was a somber day in 2000 when Greg Howit saw that he and other educators were not doing enough to save the next generation from an unhealthy and ultimately deadly lifestyle. The federal government had just released a report that detailed the rising rates of diabetes, hypertension, and heart disease—chronic diseases linked to inactivity and poor nutrition.

"I realized we had failed. As a nation we were failing," says Howit, a P.E. teacher at Don Juan Avila Middle School in southern California. "We'd been doing what we thought was a good job and we weren't."

As luck would have it, Howit was being transferred to a new school to build a quality physical education program from the ground up. He began with his own philosophy on physical fitness.

"The reason we failed was because students should've been responsible for their own health. They need to know, 'How do I get well and fit and how do I stay well and fit for the rest of my life?'" Howit says. "We needed to start relying on heart rate monitors and the ability to graph results so we could show improvement and progress. The only way we could do that was through technology."

Since then, Howit has snagged a number of grants, donations, and funds from local and national sources, enabling him, among other things, to e-mail daily fitness reports to parents.

"This is not something you just throw out there," Howit says. "We've had to change paradigms. We've managed to change the way we deliver physical education."

Data Are More Important than Ever

The value of collecting and reporting data has never been as high in education as it is now. You know the drill: Data drives decisions. But irrelevant and outdated data can be as useless as having no data. From the popular pedometer to the cutting-edge

Physical Activity in Schools

In a 2005–2006 survey, nearly one thousand respondents weighed in on their school's approach to increasing students' physical activity. Among other topics, nearly one-third noted a revised physical education curriculum.

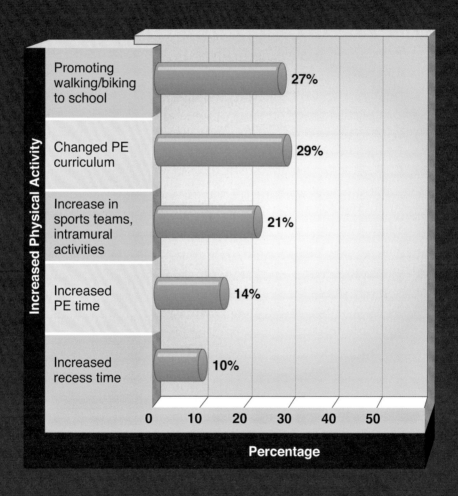

Increased Physical Activity

- Promoting walking/biking to school — 27%
- Changed PE curriculum — 29%
- Increase in sports teams, intramural activities — 21%
- Increased PE time — 14%
- Increased recess time — 10%

Percentage (0, 10, 20, 30, 40, 50)

Taken from: "Nutrition, Physical Exercise, and Obesity: What's Happening in Your School? 2005/2006 Survey Results." The Center for Health and Health Care in Schools. www.healthinschools.org.

heart monitor, devices can provide instant feedback to both the instructor and student.

"I can still remember the day and the young girl," Lawler says of a sixth-grader who ran the mile in 13.5 minutes. "She wasn't overweight or asthmatic, just not fit."

In the old days, Lawler says, he would have used a stopwatch to judge the girl against national time and distance norms. By those measurements, he would have failed her. But when he downloaded her data, the girl's heart rate registered at 183 beats per minute, rising dangerously to 207 when she ran.

"I said, 'We're getting more of these,'" Lawler says. "And you know, as we speak, there are thousands of P.E. instructors evaluating kids based on observation and they have no clue."

Heart rate monitors can be pricey, which is why the pedometer has enjoyed widespread popularity in schools. At Sterling City Elementary School in Texas, students have measured their miles in a virtual walking tour across the United States.

"We've hiked across America for the past five years. Today, we're in St. Paul, Minn., [and] by May, we'll have gone across the country," says P.E. teacher Amanda Krejci.

Krejci uses a pedometer to calculate how many steps the journey would actually take. Her students trace their progress across a map, learning geography and state facts along the way.

As the recipient of the highly competitive Physical Education for Progress (PEP) grant, Krejci used the funds to purchase pedometers and heart rate monitors, the latter of which scared her at first.

"I floundered with them for awhile; I'm not tech savvy," she says. "For the guys that are, they are running with this, but I'm struggling to use this. But I want to use it and that's why I keep trying."

Indeed, Krejci has pushed herself out of her comfort zone and tried new things like video exercise games and handheld computers, which allow her to download and view how hard students are working in real time. She says she'll try anything as long as it makes her a better instructor and helps her students become healthier.

"I think back on my years of teaching, I've learned so much," says Krejci, who has been a teacher for 30 years. "Everything was done in lines, in perfect rows, but if you come to my class today it's not like that. We are all scattered about, working on our own goals."

Exergames Motivate Students

As he strolled through a mall one day, George Graham, a kinesiology professor at Penn State University, walked past an arcade and saw a large group of youngsters crowding around a video game called Dance Dance Revolution, or DDR.

Immediately, a light bulb went off. He later coauthored a study that measured the heart rates of kids playing the interactive game, which has players use their feet to dance to popular music.

The findings were promising. "It not only looks like a workout, it is a workout," he says.

Video games have long been blamed for a corresponding lack of exercise among youth. But a new generation of video games, called exergames, may have detractors singing a different tune.

Through the use of these exergames, participants can play baseball, box, or bike the Tour de France. The possibilities are endless, exciting, and coming to West Virginia's 765 public schools. While the state's plans, the result of a multiyear study by West Virginia University, are the most extensive, West Virginia is not alone. Several hundred schools in at least 10 other states use DDR as a part of their physical education program. It's anybody's guess how many others use other forms of exergames.

Craig Buschner, president of the National Association for Sport & Physical Education, is ambivalent about the trend.

"Those aspects of technology where you can look at heart rates, count steps, and help teachers manage data collection, those are all good parts of technology," says Buschner, a kinesiology professor at California State University in Chico. "The big separation is when we step over the line, when interactive games become sort of frivolous and amusement versus having that real focus on learning and helping the teacher to manage learning."

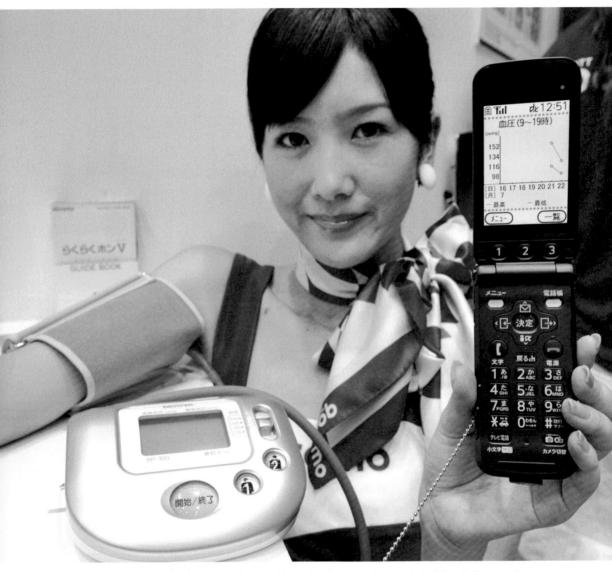

Today's technology offers devices such as this "health care" mobile phone that is equipped with various sensors that monitor blood pressure, heart rate, and other physical indicators.

But Mohnsen wonders, what's wrong with having fun? "Exercise can be boring and routine," she says. "So why not motivate (students) to move the body by playing a game? I don't see a downside to that, especially as prices come down."

Opinions are still varied, however, on the role of exergames in physical education. Toward this end, the Robert Wood Johnson Foundation has committed nearly $10 million to study how video games can improve the health of children and adults.

Still, as the price of technology comes down, new developments continue to hit the scene all the time. In addition to getting you to move, some video games now teach the proper form and technique on how to hit or throw balls for instance. Good, bad, or questionable, it's clear technology has made some inroads in physical education.

"I think about how my presentations have changed over the years," Mohnsen says. "In the beginning, I was trying to convince people to see technology as worthwhile. Now they want to know what's next."

ELEVEN

Playing Sports Teaches Life Skills

Scott Ganz and Kevin Hassett

Scott Ganz and Kevin Hassett are researchers at the American Enterprise Institute. In this viewpoint they say that people who played team sports as children tend to earn more money, get more education, and become more engaged in civic life as adults. The authors believe that children who play sports develop a strong desire for success and learn that hard work produces results. Studies show that kids take these valuable lessons into adulthood.

When pundits discuss the influence of sports on American culture, they often emphasize the negatives: Michael Vick and dogfighting; the steroids scandals in baseball; lewd fan behavior in football; doping incidents in cycling and track. But below the radar of popular athletic culture is something that has profoundly shaped the lives of millions of Americans for the better: youth sports. A growing body of research is showing the social and economic benefits of participation in youth sports to be surprisingly large and overwhelmingly positive. Other things being equal, if a kid plays sports, he will earn more money, stay in school longer, and be more engaged in civic life.

The Dramatic Impact of an Inspiring Coach

To understand how and why this might be so, consider the case of Sandy Brown, who works with the Positive Coaching Alliance (PCA), a national nonprofit organization that aims to improve the quality of youth coaching in America. As a youngster, Brown was frequently in trouble and had been kicked out of school for fighting and other unruly behavior. But Brown's life was turned around by a grade school principal and football coach named Bill Spencer. According to the PCA website, Spencer confronted his difficult new student one day and said, "Brown, I know what your problem is." Sandy thought he knew what was coming next, because he had heard this speech so many times before: *"You're no good: you'll never amount to anything."* But Spencer saw something else in the young man—potential. "Brown, you get into fights all the time because you want to compete. You have the heart of a winner."

Brown went on to play football for Spencer and had an impressive career. He is now a legendary coach at the Giddings State School, a youth detention facility in Giddings, Texas. Brown molds groups of violent young offenders into disciplined and winning football teams. Having won three state championships in the second-largest classification of the Texas Association of Private and Parochial Schools, he is regularly recruited by other "normal" schools, but feels his job at Giddings is too rewarding to relinquish.

Brown takes kids who have committed heinous crimes and gives them hope. And he does that by making the game a metaphor for life. In a speech he delivered to his players in 1997 that was recounted in a *Sports Illustrated* profile, Brown said, "You boys had some tough breaks in life. You had judges who locked you up. You had parents who kicked your behinds and didn't give you the love you wanted. But let me tell you something: What happens to you tonight is up to you. You're the only ones out here who can change yourselves for the better. . . . You've got to stand up. Do you hear me? You've got to stand up and be a man, or bow your head and be a loser."

The Long-Term Benefits of Youth Sports

Feel-good stories such as this help illustrate a larger point. An increasing quantity of research suggests that people like Spencer, Brown, and other youth coaches have a major impact on the lives of their charges. One study, by economists John M. Barron and Glen R. Waddell of Purdue University and Bradley T. Ewing of Texas Tech University, examines a series of surveys taken by American males who attended high school in the 1970s. It found that high school athletes achieved a level of education 25 to 35 percent higher than their non-athlete classmates.

It's not just educational achievement that correlates with youth-sports participation. Barron, Waddell, and Ewing also found that high school athletes had 12 to 31 percent higher wages than their non-athlete counterparts. And when the wages

Research has shown that participating in team sports has lifelong social and economic benefits.

of college graduates who were high school athletes is compared with those who were not, the athletes generally made higher wages—on average, $73 more per week. It's pretty clear that athletes win in the workplace, too.

Athletics also seems to give a bigger edge to students than other activities, such as band, student government, or theater. In another paper, Ewing estimates that, all else equal, athletes earn roughly 6 percent more than non-athletes, translating into around $1,000 per year extra wages.

Of course, it's possible that participation in athletics is just a proxy for other talents and abilities. Maybe sports do not really have a beneficent effect at the margin; perhaps it's just that more able people tend to participate in sports.

To investigate this possibility, Barron, Waddell, and Ewing also control for a number of variables in order to see if athletes are higher achievers because they share some other common characteristic. The authors examine IQ test results and standardized test scores and find that an "athlete premium" remains even after controlling for intelligence. In other words, if you take two kids who have the same IQ and put one in a sports program, he will have a better future.

Athletes are also more active citizens, a 2006 study found. Economists Mark Hugo Lopez and Kimberlee Moore of the University of Maryland examined the effect of participation in sports on civic engagement. After controlling for factors such as age, educational attainment, and income, they found that athletes are 15 percent more likely to be registered to vote, 14 percent more likely to watch the news, and 8 percent more likely to feel comfortable speaking in public (and, for public speaking, the effect on females is twice as large).

A Desire for Excellence

Why would participation in sports be associated with many benefits? Distinguished sports historian Allen Guttmann provides a clue. He notes that ancient sports were highly religious affairs, and competition was organized in order to please the gods. Modern

The Link Between Playing High School Sports and Wage Earning Later in Life

The weekly wages of college graduates who were high school athletes are greater than those of college graduates who did not play sports in high school. As the wages shown in this graphic increase, the number of nonathletes earning those wages drop off at a steeper rate than that of athletes.

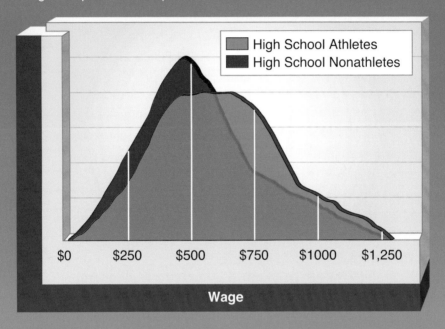

High School Athletes
High School Nonathletes

$0 $250 $500 $750 $1000 $1,250

Wage

Taken from: Scott Ganz and Kevin Hassett. "Little League, Huge Effect." *The American*, May/June 2008.

sports, however, have an entirely different character. Guttmann comments, "Once the gods have vanished from Mount Olympus or from Dante's paradise, we can no longer run to appease them or to save our souls, but we can set a new record. It is a uniquely modern form of immortality."

Small tastes of that immortality are available to today's athletes at many levels. Indeed, we speak from personal experience. What we have learned coaching youth baseball suggests why sports, especially modern team sports, can be so transformative.

For starters, one thing we have noticed is that no matter how low the stakes, the participants' emotional attachment to competition is intense. There seems to be little distinguishable difference between the transcendent joy of a World Series victor and a local Little League champion. A kid who has never had a hit in his life will feel like a Major League all-star when he rounds first base after his first line-drive up the middle. It's doubtful there is a former Little Leaguer around who doesn't rate his first home run as one of the happiest moments of his childhood.

A coach does not have to teach a kid to care about winning. Indeed, the problem is the reverse. The youth coach's role is to focus on sportsmanship, effort, and excellence precisely because the obsession over the outcome is so innate and so strong.

But since individuals care so much about the outcome, they experience—perhaps in a way that is unprecedented in a young life—a desire for excellence. Once this fire is lit, the change in the behavior of kids on a team can be extraordinary. Parents do not have to hound kids to practice. They do so voluntarily. And when they do, they almost always improve.

The positive feedback between effort and results can then lead to snowballing commitments to excellence. One particularly successful cohort in our league, for example, consisted of kids who would organize informal practices at the local ball field. If you drove past the park on the way home from work, the odds were pretty good that half a dozen 12-year-olds would be on the diamond, working out.

The Link Between Effort and Success

This lesson—that hard work can lead to excellence—is one that can transform lives. Almost all of life in a capitalist society involves some form of competition. Young athletes learn the formula for success in a market-based system. And the evidence says they outperform their peers throughout their lifetimes.

A recent scholarly paper by economists Alberto Alesina and Edward Glaeser of Harvard University and Bruce Sacerdote of Dartmouth College found that countries tend to build large welfare states when citizens believe that success in life is largely determined by luck. When citizens believe that hard work determines success, they tend to build leaner and more economically efficient governments.

Americans are remarkably different from Europeans in this regard. If you ask Americans whether the economically disadvantaged are poor because they are lazy or unlucky, 60 percent say lazy. If you ask Europeans, only 26 percent finger laziness. Alesina and his colleagues argue that these attitudes shape society by shaping governmental and social institutions.

But why do these attitudes exist? A big part of the answer may be found in sports. A 1999 study by developmental psychologists Françoise D. Alsaker and August Hammer found American children spend more time participating in athletics than Europeans. In certain cases—America compared with France, for instance—the gap is quite substantial. A 1996 study by Michigan State University sports psychologist Martha E. Ewing and Vern D. Seefeldt, former director of the Institute for the Study of Youth Sports, found that 45 percent of all eligible American youths play in an agency-sponsored league, like Little League baseball or Pop Warner football. That is 22 million children each year who get an infusion of the American work ethos.

Americans learn on the ball field or in the gym that effort and success are connected. Convinced that effort matters, we extend more effort, and celebrate and protect the fruits of effort.

Why have Americans been unwilling to build a European welfare state? Because they believe that income differences are largely attributable to effort difference. Why do they believe that effort matters? Maybe it's because they play Little League.

TWELVE

Parents and Coaches Should Be Aware of Sports-Related Concussions

Rhiannon Potkey

Rhiannon Potkey is a sportswriter for the *Ventura County Star* in California. In this viewpoint she discusses children's football injuries, particularly concussions. She discusses steps that coaches and leagues are taking to help teach students to avoid using a tackling style that can lead to a concussion. She also notes that parents need to decide whether their children should start playing football at a very young age, as the consequences of concussions can be more severe if they take place while the brain is still developing. She refers to several former National Football League players who have decided not to allow their children to play tackle football before high school.

Christian Shaifer begged his parents to let him play tackle football. But Kevin and Anita Shaifer resisted.

They felt exposing their son to so much contact at such a young age could do more harm than good.

They knew Christian had an aggressive nature and high threshold for pain and worried he may suffer an injury with long-term ramifications.

The Shaifers waited until this year [2010] to allow 13-year-old Christian to finally join the Ventura Packers [a youth football organization].

"We really wanted to find that happy medium," Kevin Shaifer said. "We wanted to start him at an age where he is more physically developed and still has the opportunity to learn quick enough to be included in high school. That was our main concern because we didn't want him to get hurt, yet we didn't want him locked out from future opportunities."

The Shaifers aren't alone in their concern.

In light of the recent revelations about head injuries in sports, more parents are asking the question: How young is too young to start playing tackle football?

Focusing on Head Injuries

New medical research has shown that successive and seemingly minor hits to the head over an extended period of time could lead to long-term brain damage. Other studies have concluded that repeated concussions can cause brain illnesses such as early-onset Alzheimer's disease, chronic depression and chronic traumatic encephalopathy.

Roughly 3 million kids ages 6–14 play tackle football in the United States.

The Centers for Disease Control and Prevention estimate there are 135,000 emergency-room visits per year for traumatic brain injuries among people ages 5–18. But it's believed many more concussions go unreported or even undetected.

The National Football League [NFL] has made a big push this season to take head injuries more seriously with stricter guidelines for dealing with concussions and larger fines for dangerous hits.

Last weekend [October 16–17, 2010] the reason for the heightened concern was displayed as several NFL players were hurt after helmet-to-helmet hits and a Rutgers University player was paralyzed from the neck down after making a tackle.

Because of its popularity and high visibility, the NFL's focus on head injuries has resulted in a trickle-down effect.

College, high school and youth football programs are taking extra precautions and implementing more guidelines to help avoid serious head injuries.

Last month [September 2010], Congress held hearings about finding ways to protect student-athletes from the risk of permanent brain damage from head injuries.

USA Football, a national governing body at the youth and amateur levels, has developed a 12-minute video about concussions and included it as part of a coaching certification exam. The organization is pushing the motto "when in doubt, keep them out" in regards to players who suffer concussions.

Although many youth league administrators say their players aren't big enough and don't hit hard enough to cause any serious damage, neuropathologist Dr. Bennet I. Omahu told Congress there is particular risk for brain injury to younger players because their brains have yet to fully develop.

"During practice and during games, a single player can sustain close to 1,000 hits to the head, in only one season, without any documented or reported incapacitating concussion," said Omahu, the co-founder and director of the Brain Injury Research Institute at West Virginia University. "Such repeated blows over several years, no doubt, can result in permanent impairment of brain functioning, especially in a child."

Leagues Are Putting More Emphasis on Injury Prevention

Moorpark Packers Bantam coach John Reilly has always been vigilant about injury prevention, but he's noticed an increased emphasis league-wide this season.

Reilly believes part of it was prompted by the death of a 10-year-old Simi Valley youth football player last year [2009] from a head injury.

David Sumner died of an acute subdural hematoma after collapsing at a football practice for the Simi Valley Vikings.

Sports-Related Concussions and Non-Sports-Related Concussions, 2008

Sports-Related

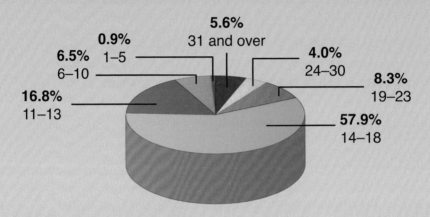

5.6%
31 and over

0.9%
1–5

6.5%
6–10

4.0%
24–30

8.3%
19–23

16.8%
11–13

57.9%
14–18

Non-Sports-Related

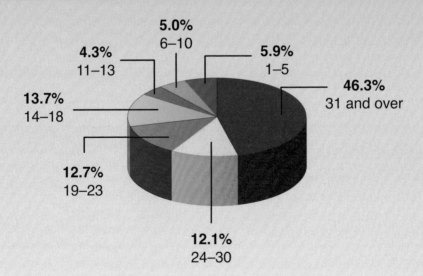

5.0%
6–10

4.3%
11–13

5.9%
1–5

13.7%
14–18

46.3%
31 and over

12.7%
19–23

12.1%
24–30

Taken from: Lan Zhao, Weiwei Han, and Claudia Steiner. "Sports-Related Concussions, 2008." Statistical Brief #114, H-Cup (Healthcare Cost and Utilization Project). www.hcup-us.ahrq.gov/reports/statbriefs/sb114.jsp.

The Moorpark Packers devoted an entire day to teaching players how to tackle properly, and showed them images of hits that caused head injuries.

Reilly makes his own players do 10 push-ups if their heads are down while making a tackle.

"It's nothing really severe, but it's to let them know they could get hurt if they [keep] doing it," Reilly said. "Tackling is something that doesn't come natural. It has to be taught. When you learn how to wrap up and do it properly, it lessens the chance of injury. Nothing can totally prevent them, but I am trying to do the best I can as a coach to keep it safe and the Packers organization has really taken extra steps this year also."

Most youth football leagues have age-group weight restrictions in place, and some have purchased newer helmets that claim to reduce concussion effects.

The local Pacific Youth Football League [PYFL] holds a coaches clinic each season that features a member of the medical profession and a representative from a helmet manufacturer, according to PYFL athletic director Verne Merrill.

The PYFL also provided coaches and players with a concussion fact sheet this season and recommended players purchase a custom-fitted mouthpiece.

The Value of Sports Outweighs the Risk of Injury

Kristyn Whittenton's son, Justise, plays in the PYFL for the Ventura Packers Bantam team. Like many mothers, Whittenton was worried about injuries when her son expressed an interest in football.

But she has been pleased with the league's emphasis on safety and would rather her son be playing football than sitting on the couch playing video games.

"You can't wrap your kids in bubble wrap and completely shelter them from everything," Whittenton said. "I have seen so many benefits from my son playing. It's been good for him socially and mentally. He has gained so much responsibility and independence and has learned how to work with other kids as a member of a team. It's not just 'let's win' or 'let's beat kids up.'"

Dr. Gerard Gioia, the chief of pediatric neuropsychology at Children's National Medical Center in Washington D.C., believes the value of sports participation can't be overlooked when discussing injury potential.

"The bottom line is that these sports overall have a better benefit than they do a cost," Gioia said. "I think the recent media attention and exposure to the issue of head injuries is good because it is really increasing the awareness that we have to take this seriously. Yet we have to make sure that we are getting the balanced message out there. Sports are a healthy and positive thing."

Ruth Gills has seen both sides. Her son, William Franklin, 20, played football at Oxnard High and Moorpark College. Franklin once suffered a concussion, but never told his mother. She found out from others.

But Gills didn't have a second thought about letting her 7-year-old son, Alonzo, play for the Hueneme Rhinos Pee-Wee team.

"There is always a little concern, but I don't have any fear about it," Gills said while working the snack bar at Hueneme High. "I think it's good for him to be out here and he absolutely loves it. I think with anything in life you do you take a chance of something bad happening, but that's not a reason to not let him play."

Football Pros Say Kids Do Not Need to Start Young

Chris Thomas spent eight seasons playing wide receiver in the NFL and knows how much pounding a body can take from football.

Thomas didn't want his son Rhylan, 10, enduring any hits before it was necessary. Rhylan played flag football last year and is taking this year off to focus on soccer.

"I looked at it from the vantage point of how much is he really going to gain from it that early," said Thomas, a Ventura High graduate and Westlake resident. "What he can learn as a skill

Current and former pro sports figures and doctors discuss the effects of concussions at the Concussions in Youth Sports panel in New York City.

position player can come without contact. He really doesn't need to be exposed to contact at his age. To me, the benefit is very little."

Thomas, 39, still talks to many of his friends from the NFL and many have the same philosophy for their children.

"The consensus seems to be they don't have a strong desire for their kids to play at a young age at all," said Thomas, who didn't begin playing football until high school. "Most of them think starting their kids in high school is good enough. They have seen how physically demanding and how violent the sport can be and have seen guys suffer a lot of injuries. They don't want to risk it starting that young."

Scott Blatt, the founder of Body Logic Sports Therapy in Westlake Village, has seen an increased level of concern from parents regarding head injuries.

Blatt has treated four youth football players with concussions at his clinic this season.

"Parents have become a lot more aware of it with so much more information out there now," Blatt said. "They are asking a lot more questions, which is great. I don't think they truly understood it before. They just thought 'my kid got his bell rung.' But now they know how serious that can be and what it can mean for their future."

A sobering reminder came earlier this year [2010] when Owen Thomas, a 21-year-old defensive lineman from the University of Pennsylvania, committed suicide. An autopsy revealed Thomas had mild stages of chronic traumatic encephalopathy [CTE], a form of degenerative brain damage caused by multiple hits to the head.

Testifying in front of Congress, Thomas' mother said, "the only possible explanation we can see for the presence of CTE is that Owen started playing football at the age of 9."

But Gioia, the concussion expert, said, "From my perspective, there is not necessarily an age issue. It is really about coaching kids properly. We know some of the old drills, when kids go up and show they are tough by popping somebody, are absolutely ridiculous. That old-school, tough-guy mentality is inappropriate and has to change. You can't put somebody at risk by doing that type of garbage."

Some Adults Encourage Unsafe Behavior

But it's apparent from attending local youth football games that players are receiving mixed messages about what constitutes appropriate behavior.

There were several "Oohs" from the crowd after a running back lowered his head and plowed over a defender. One mom in the stands yelled "Kill 'em, kill 'em" to a field of 8- and 9-year olds. An announcer increased the inflection in his voice while describing a "vicious collision."

"It's hard to get away from the fact a lot of people like the big hits in football," Thomas said. "That is part of what makes the sport attractive for some people to watch and for some guys to play. But there is a certain line that shouldn't be crossed because it can get dangerous."

For all the increased attention about head injuries, there are still many parents who are unaware of the new information being released. Many aren't sure they really want to know.

"I think for some parents ignorance is bliss in a way," said Susan Presley, whose 11-year-old son plays for the Simi Valley Patriots Midget team. "If you are constantly thinking about what could happen, it would drive you crazy from worry. You can't live in constant fear, but you do have to take precautions as a parent."

Determining what is best for their children and football is a decision parents must make individually, Gioia says. He just wants them to have the proper resources to make an informed one.

"There is no need to be scared about head injuries. What is more scary is if you ignore it and don't look at what the key issues are in early recognition and early management," he said. "Kids get better and they do well and go back to their normal selves. It is when you miss these things and kids take multiple hits and are not dealt with properly is where the real problem comes in."

What You Should Know About Exercise and Fitness

Statistics Related to Sports Participation

According to the National Sporting Goods Association, the following numbers of kids ages seven to seventeen participated in these sports in the United States in 2011:

- Baseball: 12,292,000
- Basketball: 26,095,000
- Football: 9,034,000
- Ice hockey: 2,996,000
- Soccer: 13,941,000
- Softball: 10,383,000
- Volleyball: 10,075,000

According to a study conducted by the Michigan State Institute on Youth Sports, which included a nationwide survey of ten thousand kids ages five to fourteen:

- 65 percent of those who participated in sports did so to be with friends.
- 20 percent participated in sports to improve their sports skills.
- 71 percent said they would not care if no score were kept in their games.
- 37 percent said they wished no parents would watch them play.
- 51 percent said they see other kids act like poor sports frequently.

- 90 percent would prefer to be on a losing team if they could play rather than warm the bench on a winning team.

According to the Women's Sports Foundation, female high school athletes are
- 92 percent less likely to get involved with drugs,
- 80 percent less likely to get pregnant, and
- three times more likely to graduate than nonathletes.

Facts About Obesity

According to the Centers for Disease Control and Prevention (CDC), childhood obesity, although not as severe as it was in the late twentieth century, is still a major issue. The CDC reports:
- Childhood obesity affects approximately 12.5 million children and teens in the United States (17 percent of that population).
- Obesity in children and teens tripled in the 1980s and 1990s but has leveled off somewhat since 2000.
- Studies have shown that obesity in children can lead to psychological and social problems, high blood pressure, high cholesterol, and diabetes.
- One out of three low-income children are obese or overweight before their fifth birthday.

A report by the US Department of Health and Human Services states:
- Overweight adolescents have a 70 percent chance of becoming overweight or obese adults.

Physical Activity Helps Reduce Obesity

A report by the US Department of Health and Human Services states:
- The Department of Education's Early Childhood Longitudinal Survey has determined that an hour increase in physical education per week resulted in a 1.8 percent drop in body mass index (BMI) among overweight first-grade girls.

- Outside of school hours, 39 percent of children aged nine to thirteen participate in an organized physical activity, although 77 percent participate in free-time physical activity.

The Relationship Between Physical Education Classes and Academic Performance

A 2007 study by the Center on Education Policy found:
- 62 percent of elementary schools and 20 percent of middle schools have increased instructional time for reading/language arts and math.
- 44 percent of school districts have reduced time in art, music, social studies, physical education, and recess.
- Decreasing the time allotted for physical education in favor of academic subjects does not lead to improved academic performance.
- Regular physical activity and physical fitness are associated with higher levels of academic performance and improvement to general cognitive functioning.

The Robert Wood Johnson Foundation reports on the results of a Gallup poll of elementary school principals. Key findings from the survey include:
- Four out of five principals report that recess has a positive impact on academic achievement.
- Two-thirds of principals report that students listen better after recess and are more focused in class.
- Virtually all principals surveyed believe that recess has a positive impact on children's social development (96 percent) and general well-being (97 percent).

In a 2010 review of fifty studies on how physical education affects academic performance, the CDC found:
- 50 percent of the results studied indicated a positive relationship between physical activity and academic performance, 48 percent indicated no relationship, and only 1.5 percent of the results indicated a negative relationship.
- Increased time in physical activity during the school day does not have a negative impact on academic performance.

What You Should Do About Exercise and Fitness

Gather Information

The first step in grappling with any complex and controversial issue is to be informed about it. Gather as much information as you can from a variety of sources. The essays in this book form an excellent starting point, representing a variety of viewpoints and approaches to the topic. Your school or local library will be another source of useful information; look there for relevant books, magazines, and encyclopedia entries. The bibliography and "Organizations to Contact" sections of this book will give you useful starting points in gathering additional information. Visit the websites of the organizations listed in the "Organizations to Contact" section to learn more. Do an Internet search for "exercise and fitness," "childhood obesity," or "nutrition" to find more organizations.

Identify the Issues Involved

Once you have gathered your information, review it methodically to discover the key issues involved. What are the impacts of exercise and fitness on the daily lives of children and teens? Is childhood obesity an important issue to address? How important is nutrition?

Evaluate Your Information Sources

As you learn about a topic, make sure to evaluate the sources of the information you have discovered. Authors always speak from their own perspective, which influences the way they perceive a subject and how they present information.

Consider the authors' experience and background. Are they professionals? Educators? Are they speaking from personal experience? Have they done research on the subject and gathered statistics? Someone with a personal perspective has a very different point of view from someone who has studied the issue at a distance. Both can be useful, but it is important to recognize what the author bases his or her opinion on.

Examine Your Own Perspective

Consider your own beliefs, feelings, and biases on this issue. Before you began studying, did you have an opinion about exercise, fitness, and obesity? If so, what influenced you to have this opinion—friends, family, personal experience, something you read or heard in the media? Be careful to acknowledge your own viewpoint and be willing to learn about other sides of the issue. Make sure to study and honestly consider opinions that are different from yours. Do they make some points that might convince you to change your mind? Do they raise more questions that you need to think about? Or does looking at other viewpoints more solidly convince you of your own initial perspective?

Form Your Own Opinion

Once you have gathered and organized information, identified the issues involved, and examined your own perspective, you will be ready to form your own opinions about exercise and fitness—and to advocate for that position. Whatever position you take, be prepared to explain it clearly based on facts, evidence, and well-thought-out beliefs.

Take Action

Once you have developed your position on exercise and fitness, you can consider turning your beliefs into action. Do you believe your school should be focusing more or less on physical education than it currently does? Do you think your school should take more responsibility for providing more nutritious meals? If you think there should be a change, you can write a piece for your school paper explaining why you think this. You can also arrange to speak at a local Parent-Teacher Association (PTA) meeting and explain clearly and calmly what you think.

After considering these issues, do you want to add more exercise into your own life? Are you considering changing your own eating habits? You can do more research about exercises you can do outside of school and foods that are nutritious. You may want to ask your parents if you can help with family meal planning.

You also might want to join an organization that shares your point of view—check out the "Organizations to Contact" section of this book for some starting points. These organizations offer ways that you can express your opinions or advocate for changes in school policies and procedures regarding physical education and nutrition. If you would like to contact your political representatives directly to express your position and what you think should be done, the website www.usa.gov can help you get started.

ORGANIZATIONS TO CONTACT

The editors have compiled the following list of organizations concerned with the issues debated in this book. The descriptions are derived from materials provided by the organizations. All have publications or information available for interested readers. The list was compiled on the date of publication of the present volume; names, addresses, phone and fax numbers, and e-mail and Internet addresses may change. Be aware that many organizations take several weeks or longer to respond to inquiries, so allow as much time as possible.

American College of Sports Medicine (ACSM)
401 W. Michigan St., Indianapolis, IN 46202-3233
(317) 637-9200
fax: (317) 634-7817
e-mail: publicinfo@acsm.org
website: www.acsm.org

The largest sports medicine and exercise science organization in the world, the ACSM promotes healthy lifestyles and is committed to the diagnosis, treatment, and prevention of sports-related injuries and to the advancement of the science of exercise. Its website contains fact sheets and brochures about sports medicine.

Athletes for a Better World (ABW)
1401 Peachtree St. NE, Atlanta, GA 30309
(404) 892-2328
website: www.abw.org

The mission of the ABW is to use sports to develop character, teamwork, and citizenship through commitment to an athletic code for living that applies to life and to create a movement that will play a significant role in the transformation of individuals, sports, and society. The organization provides free printed materials and a quarterly newsletter.

Boys and Girls Clubs of America (BGCA)

1275 Peachtree St. NE, Atlanta, GA 30309-3506
(404) 487-5700
e-mail: info@bgca.org
website: www.bgca.org

The BGCA's mission statement is to enable all young people to reach their full potential as productive, caring, responsible citizens. The organization offers a sports, fitness, and recreation program to youths with the goal of increasing their physical activity and strengthening interactive relationships.

Center for Nutrition Policy and Prevention

3101 Park Center Dr., 10th Fl., Alexandria, VA 22302-1594
(703) 305-7600
fax: (703) 305-3300
e-mail: Support@cnpp.usda.gov
website: www.cnpp.usda.gov

Part of the US Department of Agriculture, the Center for Nutrition Policy and Prevention's mission is to improve the health of Americans by developing and promoting dietary guidance that links scientific research to the nutritional needs of consumers. The organization's website includes the MyPlate dietary guidelines and other information on healthy eating.

Centers for Disease Control and Prevention (CDC)

1600 Clifton Rd., Atlanta, GA 30333
(800) 232-4636
e-mail: cdcinfo@cdc.gov
website: www.cdc.gov

The CDC is one of the major operating components of the US Department of Health and Human Services. The CDC's mission is to help create the expertise, information, and tools that people and communities need to protect their health—through health promotion; prevention of disease, injury, and disability; and preparedness for new health threats. Articles and fact sheets are provided online. The CDC also sponsors BAM! *Body and Mind* (www.bam.gov), an online site for kids aged nine to thirteen, designed to give them information they need to make healthy lifestyle choices.

Kidnetic.com

e-mail: contactus@kidnetic.com
website: www.kidnetic.com

Kidnetic.com is designed for kids aged nine to twelve and their families. The website includes a Leader's Guide, a lesson-based curriculum guide for health professionals and educators to use when working with patients and students; and a Parents' Guide that provides quick and easy-to-use information just for parents. The aim of Kidnetic.com is to promote healthy eating and active living in a way that is fun and relevant. The Kidnetic.com resources are aimed at inspiring kids and their families to move toward healthier lifestyles.

KidsHealth

e-mail: comments@KidsHealth.org
website: www.KidsHealth.org

Created by the Nemours Foundation's Center for Children's Health Media, KidsHealth and TeensHealth provide teens and families with accurate, up-to-date, and jargon-free health information. Medical experts post fact sheets on the website for children, teens, and parents addressing fitness, sports, obesity, body mass index, eating disorders, activity patterns for children and teens, and other topics.

Let's Move!

website: www.letsmove.gov

Let's Move! is a comprehensive initiative, launched by First Lady Michelle Obama, dedicated to solving the challenge of childhood obesity within a generation, so that children born today will grow up healthier. Let's Move! is about putting children on the path to a healthy future during their earliest months and years by giving parents helpful information and fostering environments that support healthy choices—providing healthier foods in our schools, ensuring that every family has access to healthy, affordable food, and helping kids become more physically active. Its website has information on obesity, healthy eating, and physical activity.

MomsTeam.com
MomsTeam Media, 60 Thoreau St., Ste. 288, Concord, MA 01742
(800) 474-5201
website: www.momsteam.com

MomsTeam.com is a comprehensive resource center to provide parents the information and tools they need to manage the youth sports experience. The website contains information on over one hundred topics, including sports, sports health and safety, and nutrition.

National Farm to School Network
P.M.B # 104, 8770 W. Bryn Mawr Ave., Ste. 1300, Chicago, IL 60631-3515
(847) 917-7292
website: www.farmtoschool.org

The National Farm to School Network envisions a nation in which Farm to School programs are an essential component of strong local and regional food systems. Farm to School is broadly defined as a program that connects schools from kindergarten through grade twelve and local farms with the objectives of serving healthy meals in school cafeterias; improving student nutrition; providing agriculture, health, and nutrition education opportunities; and supporting local and regional farmers.

National Women's Health Information Center (NWHIC)
Department of Health and Human Services, 200 Independence Ave. SW, Rm. 712E, Washington, DC 20201
(202) 690-7650
fax: (202) 205-2631
website: www.womenshealth.gov

The NWHIC, a service of the Office on Women's Health in the US Department of Health and Human Services, works to improve the health and well-being of women and girls in the United States through programs, education, and dissemination of health information. The center provides publications and reports on all aspects of health for women and girls.

President's Challenge Program
501 N. Morton St., Ste. 203, Bloomington, IN 47404
(800) 258-8146
fax: (812) 855-8999
e-mail: preschal@indiana.edu
website: www.presidentschallenge.org

The President's Challenge is the premier program of the President's Council on Fitness, Sports, and Nutrition administered through a cosponsorship agreement with the Amateur Athletic Union. The President's Challenge helps people of all ages and abilities increase their physical activity and improve their fitness through research-based information, easy-to-use tools, and friendly motivation. Its website contains information on fitness tests and challenges for children and adults.

Shape Up America!
PO Box 149, Clyde Park, MT 59018
website: www.shapeup.org

The purpose of Shape Up America! is to educate the public on the importance of the achievement and maintenance of a healthy body weight through the adoption of increased physical activity and healthy eating. Information about obesity and healthy diets is published on the organization's website.

Sparking Life: Power Your Brain Through Exercise
328 Broadway, Cambridge, MA 02139
(857) 221-1839
e-mail: info@sparkinglife.org
website: www.sparkinglife.org

Sparking Life is part of an international movement to reengineer school practices and medical recommendations to establish curriculum, lifestyles, and corporate practices based on scientific research that confirms that physical exercise enhances brain development, improves mental health, reduces addictive behavior, and helps maintain mental acuity. The group's website includes information about the benefits of exercise and ways that school fitness programs can enhance physical activity.

US Department of Agriculture's Team Nutrition
3101 Park Center Dr., Rm. 632, Alexandria, VA 22302
(703) 305-1624
fax: (703) 305-2549
e-mail: teamnutrition@fhs.usda.gov
website: www.teamnutrition.usda.gov

The Agriculture Department's Team Nutrition is an integrated, behavior-based, comprehensive plan for promoting the nutritional health of the nation's children. This plan involves schools, parents, and the community in efforts to continuously improve school meals and to promote the health and education of 50 million schoolchildren in more than ninety-six thousand schools nationwide. Team Nutrition's goal is to improve children's lifelong eating and physical activity habits by using the principles of the Dietary Guidelines for Americans and MyPlate.

BIBLIOGRAPHY

Books

Toney Allman, *Obesity*. Ann Arbor: Cherry Lake, 2009.

Matt Doeden, *Stay Fit! How You Can Get in Shape*. Minneapolis: Lerner, 2009.

Brian P. Geary, *Run and Hike, Play and Bike: What Is Physical Activity?* Minneapolis: Millbrook, 2011.

Lisa E. Greathouse, *Get Moving*. Huntington Beach, CA: Teacher Created Materials, 2012.

Robyn Hardyman, *Healthy Bodies*. New York: PowerKids, 2012.

Jamie Hunt, *Getting Stronger, Getting Fit: The Importance of Exercise*. Broomall, PA: Mason Crest, 2011.

Jamie Hunt, *Tired of Being Teased: Obesity and Others*. Broomall, PA: Mason Crest, 2011.

Rebecca Kajander and Timothy Gilbert, *Be Fit, Be Strong, Be You*. Minneapolis: Free Spirit, 2010.

Angela Royston, *Why Do I Run?* Mankato, MN: QEB, 2010.

Mary Elizabeth Salzmann, *Being Active*. Edina, MN: Abdo, 2004.

A.R. Schaefer, *Exercise*. Chicago: Heinemann Library, 2010.

Louise Spilsbury, *Get Active!* New York: Crabtree, 2011.

Periodicals and Internet Sources

Caralee Adams, "Recess Makes Kids Smarter," *Instructor*, Spring 2011.

Naomi Dillon, "Phys Tech," *American School Board Journal*, March 2008.

Andrew Guy, "Tackling Obesity in Black Youth," *Crisis*, Summer 2011.

Kenneth W. Harris, "Toward a Fitter Future: Why Education Must Get Physical," *Futurist*, January–February 2009.

Richard Jerome and Steve Barnes, "Childhood Obesity: The Fight Against Fat," *People*, February 12, 2007.

Jeffrey Kluger, "How America's Children Packed on the Pounds," *Time*, June 23, 2008.

Deborah Kotz, "Can She End Obesity? 5 Key Steps," *U.S. News & World Report*, August 2010.

Deborah Kotz, "It's Never Too Early to Be Heart Smart," *U.S. News & World Report*, February 2009.

Scott LaFee, "Let's Get Physical! P.E. Struggles to Make the Grade," *California Schools*, Fall 2007.

Sarah Lemagie, "Is PE an Rx for ABCs? A Growing Body of Research Says That Students Who Are More Active Do Better in School Academically," *Minneapolis (MN) Star Tribune*, May 13, 2010.

James Marks, "Improving Our Children's Health Starts Where They Learn and Play," *Huffington Post*, February 8, 2010.

Robert Wood Johnson Foundation, "First-of-Its-Kind Gallup Poll Links Recess to Academic Achievement," February 4, 2010. www.rwjf.org/pr/product.jsp?id=55248.

Evangeline Y. Samples, "Childhood Obesity," *American Fitness*, November/December 2010.

Ron Schachter, "The New Phys Ed," *Instructor*, Summer 2011.

Michelle Tan, "I'm Sick of Being Big," *People*, June 22, 2009.

Time, "Why Girls Need Gym Class," March 24, 2008.

INDEX

PICTURE CREDITS